Stoked

*On the cover: The essence of stoke: offshore winds, a zippering four-foot wave,
and a place to stand. Herbie Fletcher flying at Maalaea on Maui.
Previous page: Seaside UFOs at the Newport Wedge.
Opposite: Sliding a comber off Diamond Head, c. 1935.*

Aloha - Allan,
Tom Blake -
1991.

Angel of death. Rider unknown. Waimea Bay, c. 1960. Perilous!

Just below the point, a few yards offshore, an adventure in the wild. Burleigh Heads, Australia.

Surfing is theater, and one of the very best venues is the Pipeline at Ehukai Beach on Oahu's North Shore, where tubular drama meets the sand.

Airborne at the Banzai Pipeline, Jason Fredrico contemplates weightlessness.

Tailgate surf art defines the priorities.

Surfers are members of a different race of people from the man in the street.
—Nat Young, 1966 World Surfing Champion

Opposite: Balance of forces. Brandon Arrambide at Cobblestones in Ventura, California. Birds seem to follow him.

Second Revised Edition

07   7 6 5

Published by

Gibbs Smith, Publisher

P.O. Box 667

Layton, Utah 84041

www.gibbs-smith.com

Orders: (1-800) 748-5439

Cover designed by Robert Avellan

Interior designed by Robert Avellan

Printed and bound in Hong Kong

Library of Congress Cataloging-in-Publication Data

Kampion, Drew.

Stoked : a history of surf culture / Drew Kampion.—1st ed.

p. cm.

ISBN 1-58685-213-2

1. Surfing—History. 2. Surfing—Social aspects. I. Title.

GV840.S8 .K36 2003

797.3'2—dc21   2002015656

For John Severson, who started it all.

Stoked
A History of Surf Culture

Drew Kampion

Foreword by Bruce Brown

Gibbs Smith, Publisher
Salt Lake City

*Hot-curl crew at Mākaha, 1949:
Rus Takaki, Rabbit Kekai, Wally
Froiseth, and Roy Folk.*

Into the maw: Californian Joey Buran tests his mettle at Waimea Bay, 1980.

contents

23 foreword

25 introduction

31 the seed culture

69 the boom culture

113 from soul to pro

175 contemporary core

217 acknowledgements

218 bibliography

220 photo credits

222 index

Model and NASCAR spokesperson Becky Gordon celebrates the freedom of a longboard glide, at Zippers near Cabo San Lucas in Baja.

A book on "surf culture"—WOW!

We were always told we were a bunch of "uncultured" BOZOS! Back in the early '50s, when I started surfing, the main comment from parents and non-surfing peers was: "When you grow up, you'll realize you were wasting your time when you could have been doing something useful."

I could never figure out why golf, tennis, baseball, football or being a cheerleader was "useful" and surfing wasn't. Then the Hollywood beach movies came and that didn't help us out. They just confirmed what most people thought anyway—a bunch of surfers having food fights and drooling. Actually, we did have food fights, but we didn't drool.

I always loved the ocean and surfing and couldn't understand why everyone didn't share my views. I figured everyone would rather live in an expando trailer next to a perfect point break with no one around than in a mansion in Beverly Hills.

The other day, I ran into a guy who was rounding up some cattle. He said, "I used to be a surfer when I was a kid, but when I grew up I became a cowboy."

"That's funny," I said. "When I was a kid, I was a cowboy, but when I grew up I became a surfer." He didn't get it.

What became a "lifestyle" later was just how we lived without giving it much thought. We knew we had to live by the ocean and needed to figure out a way to make a living there. Hobie made surfboards, Gordon Clark made foam blanks, John Severson started *Surfer* magazine, I started making movies. Some guys became firemen (time off), some became teachers (time off).

Cinematographer Bruce Brown, in search of the perfect wave, 1963.

Whatever we did, the main focus was how it would affect our surf time. Getting rich wasn't important. What was important was having the freedom to do what we wanted. It didn't mean we didn't take our jobs or professions seriously; we did. It meant keeping things in perspective. After the release of *The Endless Summer,* people in the movie business would tell me, if I wanted to be successful in the motion picture industry, I would have to move to Hollywood. I said I would rather be a milkman at the beach than live in Hollywood. I wasn't kidding then, and I'm still not kidding now.

If you gave most "true" surfers the choice of moving to New York and working at an ad agency in Manhattan and making a ton of money or staying at the beach and "getting by," the vote would be: the beach.

I guess all this stuff is "lifestyle," but it takes someone like Drew to point it out to me.

I guess my answer to the question we were asked as kids—When are you going to grow up?—is, I hope, never.

—Bruce Brown, Gaviota, California, July 1997

Waves sweeping silently towards Sunset Beach during a big winter swell in December 1974.

Extraordinary

Extraordinary things have occurred in the surfing world over the last five years. Doc Ball, Miki Dora, and Rell Sunn are dead. Six-time World Champion Kelly Slater abdicated his throne. Fifty-foot waves have been ridden a hundred miles off the coast of California at Cortes Bank. A new generation of Hollywood surf films has made the rounds and come closer to the mark. Surfing is big-time, as an MSNBC financial reporter announced a "mass migration" of young people from ball sports to board sports. Meanwhile, surfing's two highest-circulation magazines—*Surfer* and *Surfing* (often referred to simply as *ER* and *ING*)—were both acquired by communications giant Primedia. It's been a big wave, and it continues to build.

As surf culture expands and extends, it also deepens its underpinning history and tradition, assuming ever-greater importance. Its cultural foundation contains mysteries that every surfer eventually wants to know. While the aim of this book is to tell the story of surfing and surf culture, it can't tell everything. The true story of surf culture includes all surfers of all eras, as well as the history of surfing in San Francisco and New York, in Spain and the Philippines, in Brazil and Japan and South Africa and Alaska. The complete history of surfing includes every wave ridden by every surfer throughout time; it includes the stories of every session at every spot, of every club and contest, of every adventure and disaster.

So this book is a beginning, a few strokes scratched onto a very large canvas—much like the series of paddling strokes that take a surfer into a big wave. Read the book, explore the images, and you'll find yourself scratching the surface of that wave. Stay with it, turn in the direction of your curiosity or desire, and find your own way down the path.

The author, watering his roots in the British Virgin Islands, 2001.

* * * * * * *

Subculture. My big fat Random House dictionary refers to it as "a group having social, economic, ethnic, or other traits distinctive enough to distinguish it from others within the same culture or society." A culture is "the sum total of ways of living built up by a group of human beings and transmitted from one generation to another." A cult? "A group having a sacred ideology and a set of rites centering around their sacred symbols." Surfing, I would discover, was both cult and subculture—the subcult of stoked.

Like thousands of surfers over the past fifty years, I rode my first wave at Malibu. It was the summer of '62, and that first awkward ride on a small wall of surging whitewater was my rite of passage, a doorway into a new world and a culture built around continual initiation.

I was not alone. I was a child of an early '60s surfing baby boom, an influx that so disgusted and oppressed the wave-riders who'd always had the beaches to themselves that some gave it up with a groan or hit the road, becoming the seeds for a further dimension of the subculture—bands of

See-through Pipeline—food for stoke!

nomadic surfers (Americans, Australians, Peruvians, Brits, South Africans, Japanese) traveling the world, forever on the hunt for perfect uncrowded waves.

As it chanced, I got into surfing at a significant point of transition in the sport and subculture—the passage from the era of the "seed" culture to an era of the "pop" or "fad" culture. It was an extraordinary moment, really. Here was a sport that had been created over a thousand years earlier by people living in an earthly paradise, a sport that was pulled back from the brink of extinction and oblivion by a joint effort of *kama'aina* and *haole* believers. Now, just as I was beginning to taste it, this same culture was suddenly the subject of a new American fad, and the beach—that outlaw zone—was becoming very popular. All of that essence that we had inherited, all of that long and hard-earned culture, was being swallowed up in the stampede to the coast. The heart of surfing was being devoured.

The sudden popularity of the sport created new pressures. Waves that had always been plentiful were now growing scarce, like a banquet to which too many guests had been invited. Surfing is not like football or baseball. You don't fence off Malibu and say that only the pros can surf here now, and you can't charge $100 to surf eighteen waves (not yet anyway), so you can't segregate it economically like the rest of our dollar-democracy. With surfing, people of all skill levels, ages, sizes, and philosophies must share the water and vie for the waves.

The pecking order was pretty wicked at Malibu in those days. The guys who'd had it to themselves in the '50s were still there whenever the waves were good—Miki Dora, Dewey Weber, Lance Carson, "Tubesteak" Tracey, "Cowboy" Henderson, Johnny Fain, and a few dozen other very good surfers. Then there were the beginners—the kooks—like me, for whom getting a good wave at the premiere southswell spot on the Southern California coast was largely a matter of luck. I didn't do too well those first couple of years.

Nursed on leftover waves in crowded summer playpens, I was nonetheless jazzed by euphoric surf tunes, whipped into a frenzy by the surf movies of the time (both the esoteric four-wall surf films and the major Hollywood sludge that so totally misrepresented anything whatsoever remotely true about my surfing experience), and stirred to poetic appreciation and longings by the equanimity and gelatinous perfection of California summertime waves.

I stood in line with the throngs on a perfect summer evening outside the Santa Monica Civic Auditorium beneath the marquis that read *The Endless Summer*. And when Terrence led Mike Hynson and Robert

August over the dunes to Cape St. Francis, and I beheld the most perfect waves I'd ever seen, I could taste them, and—I admit it—I lusted in my heart of hearts for a go at "Bruce's beauties." I was stoked.

Even today, after forty years of surfing, the smell of warm neoprene and a good sniff of a bar of coconut surf wax are all the aromatherapy I need to get focused and back in perspective. I remain thoroughly stoked.

Surfing has undergone enormous changes since I rode my first waves at Malibu. Millions now surf worldwide, a large percentage of them in places that were unknown to surfers in the '60s. Surfboards have steadily evolved over those four decades (smaller, lighter, more maneuverable), and equipment always has an enormous influence on the direction of this sport. The level of performance reflected in the gymnastic contortions of today's radical surfers would have been unimaginable in 1960, unrecognizable in 1900. Surfers spend almost as much time flying through the air nowadays as they do carving across the water. Bigger waves are being ridden than ever thought possible. In many ways, surfing has become an extreme sport, in turn stimulating other extreme sports.

Drew Kampion at Casa Severson, Maui '74.

At the same time, a living archeology is evident. The ancient *wiliwili* tree grows out a layer at a time, and when you cut it down to make your surfboard, all the rings are there, from the first year to the last. So it is with surfing. You can see it out in the water and on the beach at many of the popular surf spots today—long boards and short boards, young kids and old farts, longhairs and buzzcuts, laid-back styles of the '60s and aggressive rip-and-tear styles of the '90s.

The surf culture that has formed concentric rings around the elemental act of riding a wave is a unique and strangely powerful phenomenon. It is a subculture that feeds on the experiences and truths gained in the ocean and on the waves, and it is a subculture that has enormous effects on the larger cultures of which it is a part.

Surf culture is quite a bit like a Trojan horse. Its outward form—its energy and essential eroticism (what better natural metaphor for sex?)—makes it appealing and charismatic. Everyone wants a piece of it; it's cool to be associated with it; it's got the sizzle that makes the sell. But something else, something very ancient and esoteric, comes along with it, and when that gets loose in the culture at large—well, anything can happen. Things change. That old Polynesian seed starts to work its way into the rigid northern cultural soul and—*bam!*—people are stoked!

This book is offered to surfers as a reminder of who we are, where we come from, and how fundamentally important it is to ride waves. For non-surfers, those who surfing-great Phil Edwards once referred to as "the Legions of the Unjazzed," this book is a window into a world without boundaries—a world fed by a renewable energy source that charges its inhabitants with a fire to continually push their limitations in pursuit of ever higher levels of stoke.

Drew Kampion
Whidbey Island
1997, 2003

27

The Essence

Surfing is the deceptively simple act of riding a breaking ocean wave on a surfboard. In reality, as a fundamental physical feat, surfing on a wave is a phenomenal conjunction of forces; the mathematics of it are profoundly complex. However, as an expression of the essential relationship between man and nature, surfing is unique in its clarity. And as a metaphor for life and just about anything life throws at us, it is unparalleled. Life is a wave. Albert Einstein even said so.

Everything in the material world manifests in waves, but while the dynamics of waves modulate all phases of our existence, nowhere is this fact more graphically apparent than when man goes to sea. The most archetypal and symbolic representation of this relationship— between man and the rhythms and power of nature—is expressed in the act of riding a wave. The elemental purity of this encounter out on the ocean goes a long way in explaining surfing's almost universal appeal.

This spread: The essence of poise and balance is riding the nose of the surfboard. An unidentified rider at Fleishhacker's, San Francisco, c. 1962.

Following spread: The first Europeans were hard-pressed to understand the subtle dynamics of wave-riding as this early illustration of "The Hawaiian Sport of Surfing" demonstrates.

< The Seed Culture >

"Go to. Strip off your clothes that are a nuisance in this mellow clime. Get in and wrestle with the sea; wing your heels with the skill and power that reside in you; hit the sea's breakers, master them, and ride upon their backs as a king should."

—Jack London, *The Cruise of the Snark,* 1911

Surfboards were valued possessions and symbols of community status. In the case of the long olo surfboards used by royalty, a complex of rituals surrounded the cutting and finishing of the board. A Hawaiian homestead, c. 1825.

Out of the south they came, paddling their large voyaging canoes—twin-hulled vessels equipped with sails of woven pandanus leaves. They carried men, women, and children, and as many provisions as would fit into the boats. They brought along carefully potted bread-fruit, coconut, and pineapple plants, with pigs, dogs, and fowl. They paddled north out of their Polynesian home waters and far into the unknown regions. They crept across the gigantic equatorial waterplain with no sure knowledge of where they were going or what they would find, and when their hopes dimmed and they contemplated retreat, a huge white shark appeared and began to lead them.

The most astute sailors the world has ever known, these Polynesians navigated by stars and wind, and the patterns that wind and land and currents created on the water. Seas generated by storms radiate out in swells. If those swells encounter an island, they refract and bend around it (and also reflect off of it) as they pass. The keen observer can detect the residue of such an encounter many miles later, and these people, ever paddling north, following the migration of the golden plover, following the great shark, were keen observers of such things. According to legend, that first weary but resolved flotilla came out of the vast, near-infinite ocean wilderness of the south to draw directly upon the southern-most tip of the southernmost island of the Hawaiian archipelago, the most remote islands on earth.

< Surfing in Paradise >

The cult of surf was born in some irretrievably distant past—nobody knows where or how for sure. It is a good starting point for a surf session in the imagination. No doubt the first people who went out

Hawaiian myth and legend abound with tales of great adventures in the surf, and the first Europeans to see this incredible sport marveled at the islanders' prowess and tried to capture the complex mechanics in idealized illustrations. Maids on a Wave *by Wallace Mackay, from* Summer Cruising in the South Seas, *1874*

onto the ocean in boats quickly became aware of the inherent capacity of waves to either propel or oppose a craft. Perhaps the answer is woven into the DNA of coastal dwellers in West Africa or in Peru, where the two greatest natural powers worshipped were rainbows and waves. Certainly it is deeply seated in the essence of the Hawaiian culture.

The Hawaiian Islands are the consummate earthly paradise. Rising tall and green above white sand beaches out of a warm turquoise sea, the still-living volcanic islands were sublime, powerful, iconic, dramatic, and without a living human soul when those first adventurous settlers from the south arrived. The great peaks and archetypal monolithic rock formations, the living pits of roiling lava, the ever-present rhythmic crashing of the sea all around, the alternating breath of trade winds, Kona storms, and hurricanes—all of it yielded the subconscious images fundamental to the development of a great cultural mythology.

There is ample evidence of surfboard riding throughout the South Pacific before contact with the Europeans, but nowhere was it so significant to the culture as in Hawaii. This may have been because of the sheer quantity and quality of the waves in the Hawaiian Islands, which are situated dead center in the largest body of water on the planet, leaving them perfectly exposed to waves from all directions. Logistically and architecturally, the islands were created for surfing!

Perhaps the Polynesians who ventured so far north on their voyages of discovery were surfers who left the south in search of a fabled chain of beautiful islands with perfect waves. Whatever prompted their search, once in Hawaii, the party of explorers flourished into a new civilization. With roots steeped in traditional Polynesian values, the new culture adapted its mythology and lifestyle to these northern islands, especially in developing new ways of riding and playing in the ocean waves. As far as we know, this was the first real surf culture.

"Surf riding was one of the favorite Hawaiian sports," wrote Thomas G. Thrum in his 1896 *Hawaiian Almanac and Annual,* one of the best surviving sources of information on surfboard riding and its place at the core of ancient Hawaiian culture. Chiefs, men, women, and youth all participated, and the daily chores were put aside whenever a good surf was running. The islands' royalty especially loved riding the waves and gave themselves the privilege of reserving the better surf spots for their use alone. Wagering was common among all levels of Hawaiian society, and surfing was often accompanied by it. "Canoes, nets, lines, kapas, swine, poultry, and all other property were staked," wrote Thrum. "In some instances . . . personal liberty, or even life itself, sacrificed according to the outcome of the match, the winners carrying off their riches and the losers and their families passing to a life of poverty or servitude."

< Ritual Craftsmanship >

The construction of the surfboard was an important and highly ritualized part of Hawaiian surf culture. The most stringent rules applied to creating a royal board. When an appropriate tree was selected, a *kahuna* (priest) placed a red kumu fish by its trunk and the tree was cut down. Prayers were then offered and the kumu was placed into a hole in the roots. After this ceremony, the fallen tree was cut to the surfboard's rough dimensions, using only stone adzes or bone tools, then hauled down to the canoe shed for the final shaping with coral and rough stone. Before the surfboard was used, other rites and ceremonies were performed at its dedication.

The Hawaiian people were deeply entrenched in surfing and the powerful energy of the vast ocean that surrounded them. They had almost as many names for the types of waves and breakers as Eskimos have for snow. During prolonged flat spells, the ocean was ritually beaten with kelp and chanted to in order to "coax up" swells.

It's clear that the level of surfing in precontact Hawaii was high. In describing the practice of "surf bathing" in her mid-1800s journals, Isabella L. Bird stated that the natives rode the waves "with a slanting motion" staying "always just ahead of the breaker." Clarifying further, she said, "They were always apparently on the verge of engulfment by the fierce breaker whose towering white crest was ever above and just behind them. The great art seems to be to mount the roller precisely at the right time, and to keep exactly on its curl just before it breaks."

The Hawaiians knew how to surf at a very high level, and they crafted their surfboards in ways that revealed their spiritual consciousness as well as a profound understanding of wave mechanics and a serious appetite for having fun in the surf. Certainly, the few rare two-hundred-year-old surfboards held in sanctuary at Honolulu's Bishop Museum are scarcely enough to suggest what went on over the centuries before Cook's two-ship fleet, H.M.S. *Resolution* and HMS *Discovery,* arrived.

Olo, Alaia and Paipo

The use of long (up to 18 feet), narrow *olo* surfboards (fashioned from *wiliwili* wood) was reserved for the hereditary chiefly *ali'i,* who also claimed exclusive use of certain surf spots. Violators of this *kapu* could be put to death in unpleasant ways.

Commoner people were restricted to the shorter, wider, and thinner *alaia* boards (6 to 8 feet long) or small *paipo* boards (ridden on the belly). The *alaia* were suited to maneuvering on the waves, whereas surfing on the *olo* boards was much more of a straight-line affair.

Varying descriptions of the techniques of the early surf-riding may be traced to these differences in the vehicles and the styles of surfing appropriate to each.

Olo, alaia, and paipo boards displayed in the Hawaiian Hall of the Bishop Museum in Honolulu. Carefully crafted and hydrodynamically sophisticated, each type of board had a function and status in precontact Hawaiian culture.

< Captain James Cook >

The first island sighted by Captain Cook and the crew of the *Resolution* was Oahu, at dawn on January 18, 1778. Shortly thereafter, they spotted Kauai, then Niihau. They were at the northwest end of the Hawaiian archipelago, canvassing the North Pacific for islands while waiting for summer and a return to the North American continent to resume their search for a Northwest Passage. When a few natives ventured out in canoes to see what these strange floating birds were, Cook was surprised and delighted to hear a dialect containing the familiar sounds of the Society Islands.

James Cook's British fleet is welcomed at Kealakekua Bay, where the ambitious captain met a grisly end. Note the surfer in the lower left center.

After landing at Kauai and Niihau, Cook ventured north the next spring, eventually making it through the Bering Strait to 70° 44', where the two ships were halted by a gleaming wall of ice. Cook decided to return to winter on the Islands he'd named Sandwich after his patron back at the Admiralty. Approaching the Islands from the east this time, he struck Maui first. When the natives paddled out to greet him, he was astonished to learn that some were already clearly infected with syphilis—three large islands down the chain. Such was interisland communication. After Maui, the two boats nearly circumnavigated the Big Island, Hawaii, before anchoring at Kealakekua Bay.

Cook seems to have very much admired aspects of the Polynesian and Hawaiian cultures, notably their open friendly natures and their skill at the practice of surfing. The year before, in Tahiti, much to his amazement, Cook had seen an islander repeatedly surf a canoe. "I could not help concluding that this man felt the most supreme pleasure while he was driven on so fast and so smoothly by the sea." But even this energetic preview did little to prepare Cook and his crew for the sight of the Hawaiians riding waves on hydrodynamically foiled wooden vessels. Although this was his third round-the-world expedition on behalf of the British Royal Navy, not until the Big Island had the captain witnessed a man riding a wave standing on a board.

Even so, these Pacific islanders had their ignoble qualities, notably a penchant for thievery rooted in curiosity and an unfamiliarity with ownership. So it was them that Cook and his men occasionally shot in response to some theft or threat. This eventually wore out Cook's welcome, and he was killed in a sudden and rare outburst of self-defense at Kealakekua Bay on Sunday, February 14, 1779.

< The Dark Years >

The arrival of the Europeans brought all sorts of wonders: metal (the Islanders would trade a fat pig for a nail), guns, cannons, uniforms, venereal disease, alcohol, and a new religion. The genie was out of the bottle, and the Islands experienced a century of cultural disintegration.

The European conquistadors, explorers, traders, and racists who toured the world in the glory years between 1450 and 1800—extracting wealth, subjugating bodies, and saving souls—wielded a two-edged sword with both edges working in their favor. One edge, disease, was invisible. The other edge was the white man's religion.

The arrival of the Europeans brought cultural genocide to the Hawaiian Islands, and sunset for many of the old ways.

In the remote Hawaiian archipelago, life was simple. These people had fifty words for sweet potatoes and no word for measles; they had a dozen words for sex and no word for venereal disease. Following Cook's arrival, an estimated population of 400,000 was decimated by European viruses and bacteria until, in 1890, there were fewer than 40,000 native Hawaiians left alive, and most of them were deep in the throes of profound cultural aftershock. As the old order crumbled, surf culture, too, disintegrated.

Not only did these missionaries impose a strict Protestant paradigm on an exuberant people while diseases destroyed their bodies, but they confined them to modest attire, forced them to speak in a new tongue, and discouraged them from casual sex, gambling, and playing in the ocean. Surfing's association with nakedness, sexuality, wagering, shameless exuberance, informality, ignorant joy, and freedom were counterproductive to the designs of the church fathers, who, curiously, wound up owning most of the land in the Islands.

Mark Twain, who visited the Sandwich Islands in the mid-1860s as a reporter for the *Sacramento Daily Union,* described the missionaries as, among other things, "ignorant of all white human nature and natural ways of men." He later published a book of his travels, *Roughing It* (1872), that introduced surf-bathing to a world audience.

By mid-century, the combination of Christian training, an increasingly organized and no-nonsense job market, and diminishing numbers of native Hawaiians had reduced the sport of surfing to a rare curiosity. "Lahaina is the only place where surfriding is practiced with any degree of enthusiasm," wrote one resident of Maui in 1853, "and even there it is rapidly passing out of existence." Were it not for a few small enclaves and isolated individual practitioners, surfing might well have disappeared during the 1800s.

The Polynesian relationship to the sea was beyond European comprehension. To the islanders, the ocean meant life and joy and freedom. But by 1900, disease, religion, and a new plantation work ethic had all but exterminated Hawaiian culture and the ancient sport of surfing. This turn-of-the-century photo of a lone surfer with his short paipo board at Waikiki speaks volumes.

< The Renaissance >

By the turn of the century, the Islands had become a U.S. territory, the population of full-blooded Hawaiians had been decimated, the natives were mostly Christian, and surfing had, for the most part, vanished from the culture. About a quarter of the surviving Hawaiians lived in Honolulu on the island of Oahu, where most of the few remaining surfers congregated along the beach at Waikiki. It was here the chiefs once gathered to ride the big swells of Kalahuewehe, a spot located near Diamond Head almost a mile from shore, yet the beach at Waikiki was like no other for its peaceful beauty.

A growing number of mainland haoles (white people or foreigners) were coming to Waikiki as tourists or to live. Alexander Hume Ford, a professional globetrotter, author, and businessman, was on his way to Australia when he stopped off at Honolulu and discovered surfing. Fascinated by the sport, he dedicated his considerable personal powers to its resurrection. When Jack London and his wife, Charmian, arrived in 1907, Ford seized the opportunity. The celebrated lion of adventure literature was riding the crest of notoriety on the heels of a string of successful novels and was in high demand as a magazine writer, and Ford made it a point to introduce him to the waves and the surfers at Waikiki.

London's stirring description of the sport, published in the October 1907 edition of *A Woman's Home Companion*, included an account of his first surf session with Ford: "Out there in the midst of such a succession of big smoky ones, a third man was added to our part, one Freeth. Shaking the water from my eyes as I emerged from one wave and peered ahead to see what the next one looked like, I saw him tearing in on the back of it, standing upright on his board, carelessly poised, a young god bronzed with sunburn." The importance to surfing of the meeting of these three men at this particular time cannot be overestimated, for it marked the beginning of surfing's twentieth-century renaissance.

Stoked by London's timely appearance and passion for the sport, Ford created the Outrigger Canoe and Surfboard Club, both to secure the survival of surfing and as a way to promote Waikiki and Hawaii as "the only islands in the world where men and boys ride upright upon the crests of the waves." A flurry of hotel construction was chewing up beach frontage, and the surfers' hangouts and board-storage areas were being eliminated one by one. For $5 per year, Ford secured a twenty-year lease on an acre of beachfront and built the grass shack that was to be the first of several Outrigger clubhouses.

Three years after the creation of the Outrigger Club, another group of surfers, swimmers, and canoeists organized the Hui Nalu, a surf club whose members were predominantly Hawaiian. The Outrigger

By the early 1900s, Hawaii was attracting well-to-do travelers, who were amazed at the wave-riding of the islanders. Here, a half-dozen surfers try for a beauty off of Diamond Head in 1925.

Club was an almost strictly haole organization, and the two often went head-to-head in competition in the surf.

Formation of the clubs and the attendant publicity had a galvanizing effect on surfboarding and canoeing. By 1911, observers noted that the waves of Waikiki were starting to get a little crowded. When Jack and Charmian returned in 1915, the Outrigger Club had some 1,200 members, "with hundreds more on the waiting list, and with what seems like half a mile of surfboard lockers," wrote Mrs. London. Surfboard riding was becoming quite the local craze. Meanwhile, other seeds had been sown in California.

In the summer of 1907, George David Freeth was the best surfer at Waikiki (and, therefore in the world), and Los Angeles industrialist Henry E. Huntington was on the lookout for something to help promote his new Los Angeles–Redondo Beach rail service and the giant saltwater plunge at its seaside terminus. Hearing of the 23-year-old's prowess, Huntington hired the Irish-Hawaiian to give public demonstrations of Hawaiian watersports, especially of surfing. The event was heavily publicized, and thousands turned out to watch Freeth's daily excursions into the South Bay surf, both at Redondo and Venice beaches.

Freeth's demonstrations and the appearance of London's article happened to coincide with a new mobility (both trains and automobiles); Southern Californians were flocking to the seaside in ever-growing numbers as they gained new appreciation for the extraordinary playground at their doorstep. The combination created a new awareness of the ocean and spawned a nascent subculture of like-minded individuals.

Surf Hawaiian

Aloha: Literally, *alo* means "experience" and *ha* means "breath of life"; commonly used to mean hello, goodbye, love, mercy, compassion.

Haole: The coming of the Europeans and the handshake as a greeting created the word *ha 'ole,* meaning "without the breath of life, foreigner, white man."

He'e nalu: To surf, surf rider.

He 'ó 'la ka mea háwáwá i ka he'e nalu: The unskilled surfer tumbles (kook!).

Kaha nalu, he'e umauma: Bodysurfing.

Kahuna: A priest, a class unto itself. A *kahuna* prays for rain, abundant crops, or relief from sickness or trouble; he also uses the power of prayer for sorcery, sending evil spirits on errands of death, sickness, spirit-entrapping, and weather prophecy.

Kai emi, nalu miki: Receding wave.

Kai pi'i, nalu pú: High wave.

Kai po'l, nalu ha'l: Breaking wave.

Nalu: Surf, ocean, wave.

Nalu ha'i lala: Wave that breaks diagonally.

Nalunalu: Rough wave.

Pae: To mount or catch a wave.

Pae i ka nalu: To ride a wave into shore.

Papa he nalu: Surfboard.

Wahine: Woman, female surfer.

< Duke Kahanamoku and the Birth of Modern Surfing >

With the coming of the haole tourists to Hawaii, the loose-knit crew of surfers left behind by Freeth was enlisted to teach newcomers about waves and surfing. Among these fun-loving Waikiki "beach boys" was Duke Kahanamoku. Born in 1890, Duke inherited his moniker from his father, a Honolulu policeman who had been born in Princess Ruth's palace during the visit of the Duke of Edinburgh in 1869. The five Kahanamoku brothers lived near the beach in Waikiki and were recruited as beach boys.

Duke developed into a phenomenal waterman and athlete and is remembered today as the father of modern surfing; he also set several world records as a swimmer. In 1912, with his size-13 "luau feet" fluttering in the celebrated "Kahanamoku kick," he took the gold medal in the 100-meter freestyle at the Olympic Games in Stockholm, Sweden. Afterwards, he was feted like true royalty as he toured Europe and the U.S., giving exhibitions, swimming in meets and earning nicknames like "The Human Fish," "The Bronze Duke of Waikiki," and "The Swimming Duke."

During this time (1912–1916), Duke revealed the sport of surf-riding to the crowds on the beaches of Atlantic City and Nassau (New York), and Corona Del Mar and other California beaches. The impact of Kahanamoku, following on the heels of Freeth, was electric, as new enthusiasts took up the sport wherever Duke showed audiences how to walk on water.

Despite Mark Twain's admonition that, "None but natives ever master the art of surf-bathing thoroughly," Jack London (shown with his wife Charmian) gave it a try and published an enthusiastic account, "A Royal Sport: Surfing at Waikiki," in Woman's Home Companion *(1907). Soon, the sport was synonymous with the allure of this island paradise, and posing with a surfboard became de rigueur proof you'd been to the isles. Meanwhile, in California, three young Hawaiian princes went surfing off the mouth of the San Lorenzo River in the summer of 1885. Students in nearby San Mateo, Jonah Kuhio Kalanianaole and his brothers David Laamea Kahalepouli Piikoi Kawananakoa and Edward Keliiahonui (nephews of Queen Kapiolani, wife of Hawaii's last king, David Kalakaua) used boards milled from local redwood. However, Waikiki beachboy George Freeth (far right) is generally credited with introducing surfing to California at Redondo Beach in 1907.*

After his celebrated success at the Stockholm Games, Duke Kahanamoku was invited by the New South Wales Swimming Association to come to Australia. There, after breaking his own world record for the 100 meters (53.8 seconds) at the Domain Baths in Sydney, the Olympic champion offered a demonstration of surf-riding to the Australians, who had only recently won the right to bathe in the ocean during daylight hours.

In a "sun never sets on the British Empire" reflection of Victorian values, "sun-bathers" were required to wear neck-to-knee costumes and, where allowed, fantastic horse-drawn "English bathing machines" (little changing rooms on wheels, sometimes with built-in shark fences) were used to wheel bathers into the sexually segregated water. Except for a Tahitian boy named Tommy Tanna, who demonstrated the art of bodysurfing to a few stoked, civilly disobedient Australians in the late 1800s, the ocean was no playground until 1902, when William Gocher, the middle-aged editor of the *Manly and North Sydney News,* made good on a promise to stride publicly into the Manly Beach waters at noon on a Sunday, and damn the consequences!

Duke selected a slab of sugar pine from a local lumberyard and carved out an 8-foot-6-inch *alaia*-style board with a wide stern and a pointed bow with a slight concave scarfed into the bottom. On December 23, 1914, the board was ready, the surf was up, and Duke gave his demonstration to the throngs at Freshwater (now Harbord) just north of Manly Beach near Sydney. The conspicuously dark-skinned Olympian with the jet-black hair and huge feet surfed for almost three hours straight,

The epicenter of surfing's renaissance was Waikiki Beach, where the Outrigger Canoe and Surfboard Club (above, on the left) was founded in 1908 by Alexander Hume Ford. Thanks to London's publicity, Freeth's California demonstrations, Ford's new club (soon followed by the more modest Hui Nalu), and increased tourism advertising, surfing underwent rapid growth.

Opposite: Beach boy and Olympic Gold Medal swimmer Duke Kahanamoku was the poster boy for the 1914 Mid-Pacific Surf Carnival.

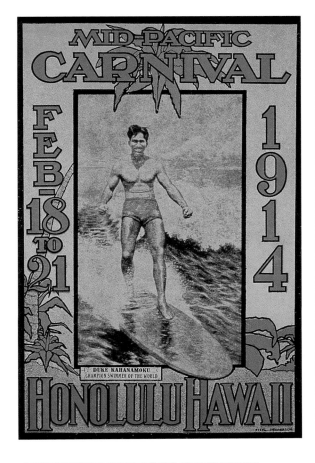

showing the Aussies every trick in the book, including the ever-popular headstand ride. He then delighted the crowd by surfing tandem with a local lady, one Isabel Letham.

And so another seed was planted. When he departed, Duke left the surfboard he built with a promising young lad named Claude West, who went on to be the first Australian surfing champion from 1919 to 1924. The water-locked continent was on its way to becoming one of the most surf-stoked societies on earth, albeit one that for years kept surfing under the aegis of beach-lifesaving authorities in a highly regimented interpretation of the "beach boy" concept.

With his good looks and easy grace, Duke also attracted attention in the world's emerging film capital, Hollywood. Over the years, in a total of seven films, he played a variety of minor roles, from Indian chiefs to Arabian princes, but never the role of a Polynesian until he was cast with John "Duke" Wayne in *The Wake of the Red Witch* in 1948. Any role the man took on seemed to fit him perfectly, but Duke's greatest legacy is ambassador for the sport of Hawaiian kings.

In 1920, Duke passed through Detroit. He and a group of fellow Hawaiian swimmers were giving exhibitions on their way home from the Olympics in Antwerp, where Duke had once again gold-medaled the 100-meter freestyle. They slipped into a theater to catch themselves on a talkie newsreel. There, a young Wisconsin lad, Tom Blake, met Duke and was so impressed by his energy and charisma that he immediately decided to devote his life to the great Hawaiian watersports—swimming, paddling, and surfing. He moved to Los Angeles and, by the fall of 1922, he was good enough

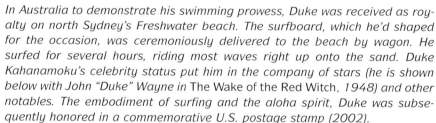

In Australia to demonstrate his swimming prowess, Duke was received as royalty on north Sydney's Freshwater beach. The surfboard, which he'd shaped for the occasion, was ceremoniously delivered to the beach by wagon. He surfed for several hours, riding most waves right up onto the sand. Duke Kahanamoku's celebrity status put him in the company of stars (he is shown below with John "Duke" Wayne in The Wake of the Red Witch, *1948) and other notables. The embodiment of surfing and the aloha spirit, Duke was subsequently honored in a commemorative U.S. postage stamp (2002).*

to win a ten-mile swim at an AAU meet in Philadelphia. In 1924, at age 24, he went to Hawaii to see Duke and, incidentally, to revolutionize surfing.

The past was all but absorbed into the Islands' volcanic heart by the time Tom Blake stepped out onto the sands of Waikiki. The population of young beach boys working the sand in front of the hotels had grown along with a dramatic increase in tourists, many of them looking to have the experience of riding a wave.

At the time, surfboards were essentially big heavy slabs of timber (usually California redwood); surfers referred to them as "planks." They were difficult to maneuver and offered poor flotation, making them hard to paddle, and paddling races were the centerpiece of the Waikiki "surf board" contests of the '20s and '30s. Inspired by an ancient Hawaiian

The population of beach boys working the sand in front of the Waikiki hotels grew along with the dramatic increase in tourists, many of them hoping to have the experience of riding a wave with a handsome young Hawaiian. This 1925 portrait includes two champion female swimmers of the day, in Hawaii at Duke's invitation. Pictured: (back row) Dude Miller, W. Nainoa, Knute Cottrall, Fred Wilhelm, Hilo Boyd, Harold K. L. Castle, David Kahanamoku, Steamboat Bill Keaweamahi, Hiram Anahu; (middle row) M. Dowd, Kim Wai, John D. Kaupiko, J. Hjorth, Joe Bishaw, William (Bill) Kahanamoku, Zen Genoves, Artie Holstein, Lewis Henderson, Sam Kahanamoku, Lando; (front row) Pua Kealoha, Ludy Langer, Ethelda Bleibtrey, Stubby Kruger, Duke Kahanamoku, Henry Prieste, H. Beckley, and H. Awana.

surfboard, Tom Blake developed a new lightweight "paddleboard" that cut previous record times by over 25 percent.

Lighter, more buoyant, and easier to maneuver, Blake's hollow board also made surfing accessible to greater numbers of people. Manufactured first by the Thomas N. Rogers Company of Venice, California, and later by the Los Angeles Ladder Company, this was the first "production" surfboard in the world.

With his many advancements in surfboard design (including the first keel or fin in 1935), Tom Blake was a catalyst for change. After a century of stagnation, a huge lightbulb had been switched on. Suddenly, anything was possible. Inspired by Blake's ideas, other surfers began experimenting with their equipment, and a design renaissance was soon underway that would turn surfing and its culture in entirely new directions.

The acceptance of Blake's hollow surfboard as a lifesaving vehicle helped popularize surfing on the mainland. Palos Verdes Estates was another popular California surfing area of the '30s and '40s. The rolling waves were perfect for styles and surfboards of the time. This photo of three surfers on their planks at Paddleboard Cove in 1935 was one of the first "water shots" taken by Dr. John Ball and inspired by the photography of Tom Blake.

Tom Blake's research on ancient Hawaiian surfboards led to the development of his hollow paddleboard. This, in turn, initiated an ongoing evolution in surfboard design that continues unabated to the present time. Left: Blake and an array of his surfboards, including three hollow paddleboards (on the right).

< Tom Blake and the Hollow Board >

Tom Blake was a good surfer and an excellent paddler. Working to come up with a faster paddleboard, he copied the dimensions of an ancient and largely ignored *olo* at Honolulu's Bishop Museum and carved a 16-foot redwood reproduction. To dry the wood faster, he bored hundreds of holes into the 180-pound board and later laminated the bottom and deck with newly developed marine plywood. The resulting 15-foot "hollow" board (built in 1926) was light for its size; it was also narrow and radically tapered in the stern, like the old-style surfboards of the Hawaiian kings.

The beach boys laughed at Blake's odd creation, referring to it as a "cigar board," until he paddled away from them; then he took it to California and won the paddling race at the first annual Pacific Coast Surfing Contest at Balboa in 1928. After developing a wood-frame construction method, he patented the "Hawaiian Hollow Surfboard" in 1930. It proved to be the consummate lifesaving tool and was soon adopted by the American Red Cross Life Saving Division, becoming the standard paddle-and-rescue vehicle at beaches across the country.

A freethinking innovator and champion waterman, Blake was a visionary surfer. Vegetarian and pantheistic, he was the prototype for an emerging lifestyle. "Tom Blake is the obvious link between the ancient South Pacific watermen and the twentieth-century Anglo watermen," says Blake biographer Gary Lynch. "Not only did he precede most other Anglo visitors to Hawaii that surfed, he understood and adopted the Aloha frame of mind . . . At the same time Albert Einstein was finishing his accepted $E = mc^2$ theory, Tom Blake was carving 'Nature = God' into the sandy bluffs of what is now Malibu. . . . We have yet to completely catch up with Tom's final footsteps."

What Is Surf Culture?

Surfing takes place beyond reach of the usual societal boundaries, so it has assumed an unusual prominence in the collective imagination. Still, there has been divergent opinion on the surfing subculture over the past 200 years. The reputation of surfers has gone from very high to very low, depending on whom you talked to and when. Early observers with a heightened sense of adventure and an appreciation for aesthetics (like Twain and London) found the "pastime" of surfing noble and praiseworthy. Calvinist and Victorian cultural ascetics (like the missionaries) found it pagan, immoral, and corrupting. Ironically, these polarities have continued to dominate popular opinion of surfing until very recent times.

As in the ancient Polynesian past, there are inherent rites of passage in the development of surfers today, and those rites of passage lead to membership at various levels within the society. Surf culture has a rich history and a unique system of rituals, distinctive language elements, symbolic elements, a loose tribal hierarchy, and unique lifestyle characteristics that have been broadly imitated and emulated around the world. Even today, aspects of surf culture express fundamental and persisting Polynesian cultural values, which regarded surfing as noble, positive, and deeply imbued with spiritual meaning.

Previous spread: Remote and desolately beautiful, the beach at San Onofre played host to the quintessential California surfing scene of the 1930s and '40s. Focused around an old grass shack and gentle waves reminiscent of Waikiki, the San Onofre crowd was able to evolve its own Hawaiian-inspired surf culture. Jam session, 1948. (Top) The tribal tradition survives: 50 years later, surfer/innovator Tom Morey taps the source in Fiji.

Left: Members of the Palos Verdes Surfing Club (founded in 1934) line up on the beach at San Pedro around a Blake-style paddleboard and its owner/builder, the great waterman Preston "Pete" Peter-son.

Below: The cover of the July 8, 1929 edition of Sport Story reflected the pre–Great Depression buzz around surfing.

< Coast Haoles >

Although Blake visited Hawaii on an annual basis, he continued to live in Southern California, where the surfing scene was growing like gangbusters. Seeded by Freeth and Duke and Blake's own hollow boards, the number of "coast haoles" (as they were referred to by the Hawaiians) swelled during the feel-good 1920s, and when the depression hit in the '30s, well, one of the few things kids without money could do was go to the beach.

By the late 1920s, there was a core group of Californians living a Hawaiian-inspired surfing lifestyle, and the epicenter of this new culture was a picturesque stretch of beach on the Santa Margarita Ranch, near the old San Onofre train station at the northern edge of San Diego County. Down on the sand, exploring surfers found a palm shack left behind by a Hollywood movie company, and it became the focal point.

By 1935, San Onofre was the most famous surf spot south of the Palos Verdes Peninsula. On a warm summer's day, the isolated beach with its rolling waves and thatch hut was a mainland Waikiki. The surfers who frequented San Onofre, sometimes camping there for weeks, created their own culture. They had ukuleles and grass skirts and palm-frond hats and big redwood boards, and soon a few paddleboards, too. A prewar neo-Polynesian golden era ensued, and the big dream was to travel to the home of Freeth and Duke.

San Onofre was the West Coast breeding ground for Hawaii-inspired surf culture. Top: The remote location was perfect for the incubation of an idyllic subculture, sustained by adventurous coast haoles who stowed away on cruise ships to the Islands and returned home to tell about it. Above: Overview of San Onofre at the start of a paddling contest in 1941.

Stowing away to Hawaii became a rite of passage for surfers right up until the era of $75 airfares in the early sixties. Even for those who never actually did it, the exciting tales of the bold few became part of the legend and lore of a sport and lifestyle that depended substantially on the "coconut wireless" for its news and information. Tales of determined young surfers pursuing their adventures on less than a shoe-string were romantic, but they also painted a picture of the surfer as a person who lived outside the boundaries of accepted society—which, to some extent, was true.

Beginning in the 1920s with the Palos Verdes Surfing Club and the Corona Del Mar Surfboard Club, surfers began to form their own associations, in part to legitimize their lifestyle. The time-consuming search for waves was incompatible with most career pursuits. One exception was lifeguarding, a natural fit pioneered in Southern California by George Freeth, who was (along with Duke Kahanamoku) famed for his many rescues. It was Freeth who inspired the rapid-response method of lifesaving now common worldwide.

But at out-of-the-way places like San Onofre, there were no lifeguards and little interference of any kind—just an idyll world of sun and surf. It was a culture in incubation, and every time surfers like Lorrin "Whitey" Harrison, Pete Peterson (the best mainland surfer of his day and four-time Pacific Coast Surfing Champion), Sam Reid, and others returned from Hawaii, they brought a little "Aloha spirit" with them. A cross-pollination was in process, and even though the "old guard" Waikiki beach crew was waxing a little xenophobic, beginning to guard its spots and ways jealously, there were big changes going on all around them.

The spirit and camaraderie of surfers before World War II was never quite recaptured again. Above: No fewer than 17 surfers share a wave during a contest at San Onofre in the summer of 1940. Below: Finalists of a 1941 surfing contest at San Onofre (left to right: Eddie Mc Bride, Vincent "Klotz" Lindberg, Don Okie, Dorian Paskowitz, Jim Bailey, Lorrin "Whitey" Harrison, Tom Blake, Pete Peterson (winner of the contest), Slim Van Blom, Davie Williams.

Surf clubs were an integral part of the pre-war surf scene. Below: Santa Cruz was an early outpost of California Surf culture: the Santa Cruz Surfing Club in the late 1930s. Right: Palos Verdes guys join the locals at Curries in Hermosa Beach to celebrate the end-of-the-war summer of '46.

<The Hot-Curl Surfboard>

The reappraisal of surfboards that followed the development and patenting of Blake's hollow paddleboard almost immediately transformed the very nature of surfing. An immense paradigm shift was occurring. Instead of reverently reproducing old Hawaiian designs, there was a new attitude of exploration and experimentation reflected in a series of small but ultimately revolutionary events that changed the character of surfboards and, in the process, the way surfers surfed.

One of those incidents occurred at Brown's Surf, a spot on the opposite side of Diamond Head from Waikiki. John Kelly, Fran Heath, and Wally Froiseth were surfing 15-foot waves there one afternoon in 1934 and were having trouble with the classic wide-tailed planks. Whenever they turned to slide along a hollow wave, the tails of their boards would sideslip, a characteristic of finless boards known as going "slide ass."

Frustrated, the surfers came back to the beach, where Kelly took up an axe and whittled the tail down to a narrow 5 inches, tapering the bottom into a vee-shape. The result was incredible. "I caught a wave and the tail just dug in, and I went right across, and we figured something had happened," Kelly recalled ("Hot Curl," *The Surfer's Journal,* Vol. 3, No. 2).

The new boards were called "hot curl" boards because they allowed much faster and more radical surfing in the hollow curl of the wave. Increasingly modified and refined, hot curl boards turned out to perform better as the waves got bigger. In a clear example of technology leading the way, Froiseth, Kelly, and a handful of others took to hunting big waves on the north and west shores of Oahu, where they could explore the possibilities of their new equipment without getting "stink-eye" from more conservative old-guard surfers, who preferred a more rolling surf and a trick-oriented style.

The hot-curl surfers rode shorter, more streamlined boards that had traction on the turns; they could ride high and fast up in the "pocket" of the wave. Hot-curl surfing was the beginning of "hotdog" surfing, and the masters of the art (Rabbit Kekai, Blackie Makahena, Mongo Kalahiki, Scooter Boy, Dickie Cross, Woody Brown, and a kid named George Downing) were the harbingers of things to come.

The narrow-tailed hot-curl boards called for a whole new style of surfing, and Blackie Makahena (shown here at the Waikiki spot Canoes in 1950) was a sublime practitioner. Below: Surfer *magazine editor Sam George hoists a well-preserved specimen; the hot-curl's aft-end vee-bottom held it in the wave, a function handled by the fin beginning in the early 1950s.*

Left, top to bottom: The Roosevelt Highway opened the Malibu coast to new generations of surfers. Overview of Malibu Point and pier, 1947 — post-war ground zero for development of the modern surfboard. Riding Bob Simmons balsa concaves, Dave Sykes and Peter Cole slide Malibu in the summer of '49. Above: Malibu was the place to be in the summer of '51. Left to right: Don Drazen, Bill Stevens, Robin Grigg, Dave Rochlen, Peter Lawford, Tom Carpenter, Molly Dunn, and Tim Lyons. These kids had the look and attitude that defined modern surfing in the second half of the 20th century.

< The Malibu >

About the same time that San Onofre was beginning to attract surfers, another new spot was discovered just north of Los Angeles—a jutting wedge of sand and cobblestone that faced south towards the approaching summer swells. If San Onofre was a place that celebrated surfing's Hawaiian roots, Malibu was destined to become center-stage for the new creative edge of the sport. Eventually, and ironically, it would also prove to be a wellspring of surfing's mystique mass-market appeal.

Up to the time Tom Blake, Sam Reid, and Duke first surfed there, the entire Malibu coast had been the exclusive domain of Samuel K. Rindge, who had worked to preserve the integrity of the old family land grant. His strong and determined widow, May Knight Rindge, fought to stop a federal highway along this idyllic stretch of points and coves, once the sacred home of the Chumash and Gabrielino peoples. In 1925, despite her lawyers and armed cowboys, the battle was lost, and the state won its eminent-domain lawsuit. In 1926, construction on the Roosevelt Highway (now a stretch of State Highway 1) began, literally paving the way for the opening and development of the Malibu coast.

Legal access to the coast along Rancho Malibu remained limited to private use and those with business on the land. However, a stretch of shoreline north of Malibu Point, called Malibu Colony, was sold to the Marblehead development company, and it was here that the stars met the sea. Ronald Coleman tried his hand at surfing the Malibu waves, as did Jackie Coogan, Joel McCrea, and a parade of other surf-stoked Hollywood celebrities over the years.

Word of the perfect Malibu waves spread, but with the Rindge guards still manning the gates and fences, getting to them was a case of who you knew or how bold you were. Pete Peterson was one of a lucky few. His girlfriend worked at the Marblehead tile factory, about two miles south of Malibu Point. When the swell was running, he would drive her to work, slip through the fence with his board, and walk up the beach to surf the point alone. The price of such incursions was eternal vigilance. Two other early Malibu pioneers, Dave Rochlen and Joe Quigg, having made their way several miles into the heart of the Rancho, found themselves hiding behind the rocks at Sequit Point (now Leo Carrillo State Beach) under fire from Rindge cowboys.

Over the years the Rindge estate was sold off piece by piece, in some cases to the state. Malibu Point, between the Colony and the pier, was opened to the public (and later named Surfrider Beach); it was the place to be when summertime south swells swept into the coast.

The few surfers who had enjoyed the place alone would soon be joined by others, and others still. Malibu would become the scene of a new kind of surf culture, one based on individual identity sculpted out of performance and style. It would become very tribal, territorial, and exclusive, and then it would become very Hollywood.

But first—just then—along came World War II, which put an effective stop to the powerful peacetime momentum of surfing, both in Hawaii and on the mainland.

One of the unsung stylists of the early Malibu era, Dick Barnard was a pilot who died tragically young. Clean, glassy Malibu walls, like this one in the summer of '51, provided Barnard, Les Williams, Gard Chapin, Tom Zahn, and others with perfect waves on which to develop their own stylistic nuances, ushering in a new era of performance surfing that would rock the world.

< Planing Hulls, Potato Chips and Pigs >

Bob Simmons (left) holding forth at Windansea with Tom Carlin, Jim Nesbitt (a naval aviator), and Johnny Fain. "This was January 9th, 1954," John Elwell recalls. "The surf was so big we could not get out at the Sloughs. Windansea was breaking in long lines from point to point in the kelp beds. Simmons tried to get out in a lull and a monster set came in, and he rolled through ending upside down holding onto his rope handles." In September, Simmons would drown there.

John Elwell recalls: "Simmons' car, a 1937 tudor with a V-8 60hp engine. Bob had stripped the driver's seat out and painted out the rear windows, took out the rear seat and trunk wall. He plywooded it in and slept back there with his feet stretched out into the passenger area. He had cans of soybeans, with fresh fruit on the floor boards, oceanographic charts of Southern California and the world in the back, with his boomerangs. His bathing suit, a woolen World War II navy-surplus-type was hooked on the front bumper to dry while he drove to the next surfing spot. He always had Ping-Pong paddles aboard. He had a string of paper-encased wooden ice-cream spoons to eat with and a can opener. He never carried a change of clothes and smelled like it. He only bathed while surfing and was always sea-salt encrusted. His clothes were covered with fiberglass and resin, that smelled as such, blended with body odor. He had permanent surf board racks bolted onto the roof. The board shown on top is his 'latest machine,' a concave, dual-finned, hydrody-namic, slotted-nose and -tail board with roll handles—a favorite 11-foot board for the biggest days and the finest of Simmons' designs. Note the thin rails! The board disappeared after his death."

During World War II, beaches were borders, fortified and monitored from every point and headland, as invasion fears swept the shores clear. Surfing—along with most of life—entered hiatus. With most young men in uniform, the only people near the beaches were a few kids, some military personnel, and a handful of surfers with special situations.

One of them was Robert Wilson Simmons, a young man who'd begun paddling a Tom Blake paddleboard in 1939 as therapy after a near-fatal bicycle accident crippled his left arm. A brilliant mathematician with a scholarship at Cal Tech, Simmons worked as a mathematician for Douglas Aircraft, but got so surf-stoked he'd quit his job when the waves were good and go back when the swells died down.

By the end of the war, Simmons was focusing his considerable technical skills on surfboard design. Taking an analytic approach to the complex problem of wave-riding, he integrated the nascent hydrodynamic theo-ries of naval architect Lindsey Lord with newly developed fiberglass technology to create an improved generation of redwood boards that were stronger, more streamlined, and faster. Simmons referred to them as "hydrodynamic planing hulls." Subsequently, he developed his famous "sandwich boards" (fiberglass skin, plywood deck and bottom, balsa rails, Styrofoam core) and glassed balsa boards, which employed such radical design innovations as concaves and twin fins.

What Simmons achieved in tech-nical knowledge, he lacked in interpersonal skills. A restless loner with no patience with the post-war influx of novice surfers, Simmons (along with his friend Gard Chapin) introduced a spirit of offbeat elitism that hardly had precedent and would soon become central to the Malibu surfing experience—surfers who positioned themselves as rebellious outsiders, inchoate individualists who felt that what they were doing was on a different plane than the unini-tiated masses.

In September 1954, while surfing a good-sized swell at Windansea in San Diego, Simmons slipped on a late takeoff and failed to surface. His body was found three days later.

A contemporary of Simmons, Joe Quigg was one of many prominent surfers to graduate from Santa Monica High School. Born in 1925, he'd surfed nearby Malibu since '39. After serving in the Navy, he bought a Simmons redwood but eventually decided to build his own boards out of balsa, which was much lighter and easier to shape.

Lifeguards: Towers and Fashion

Surfing and lifesaving go hand in hand. Surfers know the ocean and its moods like no other part of the population. Since the days of George Freeth and Tom Blake, a large number of surfers have spent a lot of time in lifeguard towers. The first tower was, in fact, designed by Long Beach surfer/paddler/doryman Bill Butz in 1933. In the beginning, since they were completely uncovered with the lifeguards exposed to the sun and elements, the raised platforms were referred to as "penalty boxes." Later, out of compassion, an umbrella was added; then in 1944 an architectural student (Butz again) designed a tower with a cover and ramp, similar to the ones common today.

In the postwar years, being a lifeguard was considered good duty and was locally prestigious. In fact, it was lifeguard "fashion," says *Surfer* magazine founder John Severson (himself a guard on the beach in San Clemente in the mid-'50s) that planted one of the seeds of the surfwear industry. "As lifeguards," he recalls, "we got to pick our trunks for the year. Sometimes they had little white stripes down the side or something, and the other people on the beach would look up to the lifeguards and their trunk style, and that was like the beginning of surfwear."

Lifeguarding remains one of the few jobs that will keep a surfer in sight of the waves. The thousands of rescues surfers have performed over the decades have helped to keep these free spirits on the good side of those who might otherwise be repelled by their sometimes-antisocial behavior.

Lifeguardin' at the San Clemente pier, John Severson hams it up in the summer of 1951.

Larry Baily (right) helps Dale Velzy hog out a balsa "blank" — the rough-shaping stage of forming a surfboard. Balsa was much easier to work with than redwood or any other earlier construction material and expedited the growth of the sport: boards could be made faster and better with less training. It was Velzy who saw the potential, opened a surf shop (with Bev Morgan and then Hap Jacobs fiberglassing) and got the Hermosa kids into surfing his boards. He called them his gremlins, and the term stuck, morphing into "gremmies."

Quigg's balsas were beauties. He made an effort to select the lightest clearest wood, glassed them with clear resin, then attached fiberglassed white pine fins. They averaged 9 feet 6 inches in length and weighed between 25 and 30 pounds. In June 1950, Quigg recalled, "A gang of Malibu guys went down to Windansea, and the San Onofre guys were down there, too. It was raining, so we took our boards out and slept in our cars. When the San-O guys woke up and looked out of their cars and saw our boards laying around, one of 'em called out, 'Hey! It looks like a bunch of potato chips!' And that name stuck."

In 1952, South Bay surfer Dale Velzy was inspired by a particularly nice Quigg pintail to try shaping one himself. Within a few months he'd rented a shop up the street from the Manhattan Beach Pier; he was shaping balsa surfboards up front, Bev Morgan glassing them in the back. Velzy's philosophy of surfboard design was simple: "I try to make boards as easy to surf as I can. Instead of taking two years to learn to surf, with the chips it would take four weeks." With creative designs like his "pig model," Velzy soon had more business than they could keep up with, and his shop (the first such retail establishment for surfers) became the center of a South Bay surf culture in the late '50s.

With their deeper fiberglass fins, a more rounded outline shape, and "rocker" or lift in the nose and tail, the lightweight potato chip (or Malibu chip) boards became the vehicles for a whole new style of "hotdog" surfing. They were so maneuverable they could be ridden in the dumping, near-shore beach-break waves that were by far the most prevalent sort of surf in Southern California. They magnified the surfable terrain and proportionally increased surfing's exposure. Suddenly surfing, which had been practiced largely at a few remote spots, was happening at beaches everywhere.

It all came together at Makaha in the late '40s and early '50s, when the potato-chip Californians met the hot-curl Hawaiians. The resulting fusion of equipment and performance style resulted in an exciting new hybrid form of surfing. Top: Makaha winter quarters with Leslie "Bird Man" Williams and Buzzy Trent in the doorway and a woody out front. Top right: Bob Crane in the cabin, boards hanging in the rafters. Middle: The Makaha crew, c. 1950. Bottom: Big-wave surfer Walter Hoffman and wheels near Makaha in '49. Scion of the Hoffman Fabrics family, he began designing Hawaiian print shirts in the early 1950s.

< Makaha at the Crossroads >

After the war was over, surfers once again shuttled back and forth between the mainland and Hawaii, but now there was a new island mystique. On December 22, 1943, frustrated with the lack of surf around Waikiki, Woody Brown and Dickie Cross had paddled out through the rip at Sunset Beach on Oahu's North Shore. A big day got bigger, and they were caught in a rapidly building swell. It was the biggest surf in years—30 feet or more. Woody was a relative veteran, Dickie less experienced, but neither had much big-wave experience.

Drawn farther and farther outside to avoid the increasingly lethal avalanches, they decided to paddle the five miles down the coast to the deep water of Waimea Bay and come ashore there. But Waimea was closed out, and monster waves thundered across the mouth of the bay. In the ultimate surfing horror story, the horizon went black with the largest set yet, and the two surfers were caught inside. Woody was finally washed onto the beach, but Dickie was never found.

The death of Dickie Cross kept surfers away from the "heavies" of the North Shore for more than a decade. Some said Woody Brown never paddled out into the big stuff after that, but Walter Hoffman saw him ride the biggest wave he ever saw anybody ride. It was around 1950, and it was at Makaha.

Makaha, on the west side of Oahu, somehow seemed safer than the North Shore, even though the surf could be giant here, too. A golden curve of beach on the arid leeward shore, the place was almost desolate in the late '40s and few surfers went there. Mostly it was just the hot curl guys—Wally Froiseth, George Downing, Woody, and a few others—whose streamlined boards loved the big wave faces as much as they did.

Makaha was paradise—hot and dry with offshore winds day after day. The surfers camped, fished, and surfed. It was the original "country" life, and the beginning of the annual California-to-Hawaii winter big-surf migrations. Walter and Flippy Hoffman, Buzzy Trent, and a growing number of others joined the "town" surfers who made the regular drive out to the West Side. Together they'd drink beer, sing songs, and talk stories.

The mix of town and country and of *kama'aina* (Hawaiian-born) and haole surfers at Makaha brought a new energy to surfing. It was different from the sport as practiced at Waikiki. Makaha was a wild place that seemed to evoke the long-ago spirit of the Polynesian roots of *he'e nalu*. The ancient gathering place was once again becoming a center of surf culture, and in the winter of 1954 the first Makaha International Surfing Championships were held there, combining surfing, bellyboarding, paddling, and tandem surfing events. George Downing was crowned champion, and photos of the big waves at Makaha made the mainland papers.

In 1952, Greg Noll, Jim Fisher, and Mike Stang dropped out of their California schools and headed to Hawaii. Shortly after seeing a photo of big-wave surfing on the front page of a San Francisco newspaper, Fred Van Dyke quit his teaching job in Santa Cruz and followed. His friends Peter Cole and Ricky Grigg left Stanford University to chase big waves with him. Soon Fred's brother, Peter, Pat Curren, Warren Harlowe, Jose Angel, and many others joined the migration. It was the twilight of surfing as sport of a relative few. The surf cultures of California and Hawaii were cross-pollinating at a time of isolated stoke and shared ideas that seemed like it would last forever.

Three pioneers of the "chip" surfboard—Joe Quigg, Matt Kivlin, and Tom Zahn—leaving Honolulu for Los Angeles on the Lurline, March 1948. Quigg was the prime synthesizer of the Malibu surfboard; Kivlin was perhaps the finest Malibu stylist of the early '50s, and Zahn was an archetypical waterman, a lifeguard and prodigious paddler, who completed a rugged 36-mile channel crossing between Molokai and Oahu in 1953.

Left: "The Queen of the Coast," Rincon Point is the premier winter surf spot in Southern California—as good or better than Malibu and often providing more powerful waves. This photo was taken in 1947 by Joe Quigg, who recalled: "This picture and the beautiful wave at Second Point inspired me to build the first super-light, narrow surfboard with extreme low rails, tail rocker, rail rocker, and the first deeper all-fiberglass fin. I called it a 'modern speed board.' Years later, Buzzy Trent called that type an 'elephant gun' or 'gun' for short. In the '60s, the kids started calling them pintails." Bob Simmons' car is parked on the roadside with his board on the roof.

BUD BROWNE'S

7TH ANNUAL SURFING FILM

Cat on a Hot
Foam Board

Two early masters of surf photography: "Doc" Ball and Bud Browne. John Ball was inspired by Tom Blake to take photographs of surfing using a waterproof camera; as a result, he documented an era and is remembered as the Ansel Adams of surf photography. This photo of him (above) at Paddle-board Cove around 1938 was taken by Blake. Surf-movie pioneer Bud Browne (right) fanned the flame of surf stoke throughout the 1950s and '60s. Here he's ready to go to work at Makaha in 1962. Browne toured the coasts with Cat on a Hot Foam Board in 1959.

< Photography and Early Surf Movies >

"The real unsung hero, the man always in the background of surfing is Bud Browne," wrote Fred Van Dyke in *30 Years of Riding the World's Biggest Waves.* "While the heroes are carving their names in the Surfing Hall of Fame, Bud is the photographer, bedecked with camera, wetsuit and fins, who sits hour after hour at the impact zone. He goes over the falls, shooting film of the surf heroes."

Bud Browne was the first of a long line of cinematographers to translate the exciting, often terrifying, and always beautiful and compelling dance of surfers and waves into movies for viewers far away. Although Dr. John Ball had made an interesting 16mm film, *Californian Surfriders,* in the mid-'40s, it was Browne's films, beginning in 1953 with *Hawaiian Surfing Movie,* that systematically fanned the fires of surf stoke year after year. It was the "surf film," combined with the lightweight balsa boards, that gave surfing its big growth spurt in the mid-'50s.

Browne, an outstanding waterman in his own right, not only provided the first widely circulated images of hot surfing action, he created the first real vehicle for fame. Surfers known only at their own beaches or who were merely rumored entities, like gods, could now be seen, admired, and emulated.

Taking his one-man show (he filmed, edited, publicized, took tickets, narrated, and swept up) on the road, Browne paved the "four-wall" circuit, showing his films in school auditoriums and small halls along the California coast, making stars out of surfers like Downing, Froiseth, Buzzy Trent, Jim Fisher, Peter Cole, and then Phil Edwards, Mickey Muñoz, and Mike Doyle. He aroused more and more surfers with the scent of Hawaii and the "heavies."

Browne's films combined small-wave hotdogging and big-wave thrills with lifestyle, from on-the-road "surfari" sequences to intricate gag scenes. His formula became the model for a hundred other filmmakers who followed in the late '50s and '60s.

Off to an earlier start, surf photography grew alongside the sport throughout its twentieth-century development. Beyond the occasional photograph or illustration in early magazine narratives or books, like those by Twain and London, few images of the early Waikiki surf scene had been circulated. But in 1929, Tom Blake bought a 4 x 5 Graflex camera from Duke, created a waterproof housing for it, and took a number of excellent shots of Waikiki surfers from his paddleboard. The stunning results, published in a 1935 edition of *National Geographic,* not only alerted a much wider audience to the thrill of surfing, it inspired several young people to take up cameras, among them two California surfers, Dr. John H. "Doc" Ball and Don James. Beyond these two, most of the still photography of surfing done before 1960 was in the form of snapshots taken by amateurs or by the occasionally curious newspaper- or magazine-feature photographer.

James, who was from Santa Monica and hung out around the Del Mar Beach Club, was immediately inspired by Blake's photos. "I began shooting pictures to show our parents and teachers what was going on," he told artist and surf historian Craig Stecyk just prior to his death in December 1996. In the end, James' body of work spanned six decades of surfing history.

Down the coast a few miles at Hermosa Beach, Doc Ball started taking pictures at Palos Verdes from his paddleboard, first with a Kodak Autographic folding camera and later with a Graph-Light. He had to reload after every shot, sitting out there on his paddleboard. "You had to keep an eye on what you were doing," said Ball, whose photographs of the surfers at Paddleboard Cove, San Onofre, and other spots along the coast established him as the Ansel Adams of surf photography.

All of this exposure had a price, however, and over in Hawaii it was becoming more apparent with each passing season. "Crowds came to the North Shore—or what we considered crowds—about twenty new guys in all in 1956," wrote Fred Van Dyke. "Everyone had one purpose in common, to ride and conquer his fear of the North Shore."

Surf photographer Dr. Don James was also inspired by Tom Blake to beautifully document mid-20th-century surf history. He was on hand to capture the action on the first day Waimea Bay was surfed (right). Above: James shooting the action at Makaha in 1962.

Spinning Boards *was Bud Browne's 1961 film; the artwork for the poster was done by a young artist named Rick Griffin.*

< Waimea Bay >

Top: First day at the Bay. After years of fears and the echo of the frightening loss of Dickie Cross, Waimea was finally attempted and successfully ridden on November 7, 1957. One of the first "heavies" was ridden by (left to right) Greg Noll, Pat Curren, Del Cannon, and Mickey Muñoz (wiping out).

Inset: The first-day crew included (left to right) Greg Noll, Mickey Muñoz, Bob Bermell, and Mike Stang. On that day, the brotherhood of big-wave surfers took a giant step forward.

One of surfing's archetypal images is a giant wave at Waimea Bay. On a summer's afternoon on the North Shore's golden sand and emerald coastline, this picturesque scoop of azure cove is a placid jewel that invites a lazy swim or a dive from the big rocks on the outer edges of the small bay. But come November, December, and January, it's a completely different story.

When big winter storms pinwheel across the northern Pacific towards the Aleutian Islands, they whip up giant swells that rise up, darken, and roar over in thundering pulses. When the waves are big enough, say twenty feet or more, most spots "close out," breaking on the outer reefs, far outside of the usual spots, and, in the 1950s and '60s, few seriously considered riding out there.

But there was one spot that stayed "open" in the huge surf: the deepwater bay at Waimea. Here the waves would march in and stack up off the point, throwing up a large clamshell peak with a some-times-sloping shoulder that tapered into deep water at the center of the bay, offering at least the possibility of an exit to a surfer who might successfully catch one.

Each winter, Greg Noll drove over from Makaha, passing Waimea on his way to surf Sunset. Occasionally he would exhort his big-wave buddies to join him in an adventuresome foray at the Bay, but they weren't going for it. "We'd looked at it for three years," Noll said in an interview. "Everybody was spooked by the place—the ancient Hawaiian *heiau* [place of worship] on the hilltop, the old house below was supposed to be haunted, and then Cross getting killed there. . . . No doubt about it, the place had major mystique. You had to believe with all that bullshit flying around about the place that if you went out there you'd paddle into some big hole and get swallowed up or something. Buzzy Trent was calling me the pied piper, and saying that we'd drown like rats."

But on November 7, 1957, it finally happened. "We were driving out toward Sunset," Noll recounts, "and we stopped at Waimea. It was a clean day, not huge, maybe eighteen to twenty feet, and it was me and Mike Stang, and we just looked at each other and said, let's hit it. So we paddled out, and then I looked back and Pat Curren and someone else was paddling out."

Noll claims to have ridden the first wave, though accounts vary; some say it was Harry Schurch. Noll explains: "It was a small set, and I took off on the shoulder, dropped and pulled out. The sky didn't part, the Hawaiian gods weren't pissed, I was still alive. By this time Pat and Mike were out there, and they got the next wave, and then I looked in and there were guys rippin' their boards off the cars! The taboo was broken. Twelve guys probably surfed it that day."

Noll recalls that the local people, who feared the place and warned the surfers not to surf there, suddenly appeared. "Almost the entire town of Haleiwa emptied out! 'Cuz the crazy haoles were gonna commit suicide at Waimea Bay!"

The conquest of Waimea Bay electrified the surfing community. This was surfing as an extreme sport, and you didn't have to be an aficionado to appreciate it. Watching Greg Noll (the big haole in the black-and-white striped trunks) drop over the cornice of a 25-foot-high Waimea wall with nothing but air underneath him either made you shake with fear or want to get over there and try it.

< Meanwhile, Down Under >

Surfing in Australia had taken a curious evolutionary path since Duke Kahanamoku carved that first surfboard and gave his demonstration of the sport of Hawaiian kings in 1914. The history of surfing on this southern continent was largely the history of the surf-lifesaving associations. While surfers continued to ride plank clones of Duke's pine board, the lifesavers developed beautiful surf boats (dories), surf skis, and an elaborate calendar of surf carnivals centered around competition between the surf-lifesaving clubs. Australian surfing had remained a primitive and minor component of a complex system of institutionalized bathing, calisthenic beach safety, and grandiose public display.

Although actor and Malibu surfer Peter Lawford had brought a balsa chip board along on a film shoot to Australia in 1952, no one seemed to notice. But two years later, stimulated by some bureaucratic interest in surf-lifesaving, the U.S. government sponsored a mission of top American paddlers to Australia, coincident with the 1956 Olympic Games in Melbourne.

Led by Tom Zahn, the team of California lifeguards included Bob Burnside, Bob Moore, Mike Bright, and Greg Noll. They competed on paddleboards at surf carnivals up and down the eastern Australian coast, but they'd brought their Malibu chips, too. One afternoon, after racing at Torquay, Bright and Noll spotted a likely looking peak and paddled out.

The Sydney newspapers announced the arrival the U.S. "lifesavers" for the 1956 surf carnivals at Avalon, Cronulla, and other beaches. This photo of Greg Noll (right) and crew made the front page. The arrival of the Yanks shattered the Australians' rather stodgy idea of the sport and precipitated a revolution in "Malibu-style" surfboards (or Mals) in the late '50s. With the arrival of the "foamies" of the early '60s, Australian surfers jumped on the bandwagon and created clubs, competitions, and lifestyles that were very reflective of the American surf scene that was suddenly coming their way in movies and magazines. Top: These flamboyant Aussie surf cars were owned by John Arnold and his Adelaide mates.

"I remember taking a wave," said Noll in an interview. "I made a little turn and cut out the back, then I looked up and saw these people running up the beach. I thought somebody had a heart attack." The crowd had seen Noll and was responding to a kind of surfing they'd never seen before: Malibu-style hotdogging on maneuverable boards.

"Our boards blew the whole thing away," Noll summarized. Event-sponsor Ampol Oil filmed the surfers and, after they left, circulated movies to surf-lifesaving clubs around the country, where it had a catalytic effect. Balsa was hard to get in Australia at the time, so the top Australian board makers (like Bill Wallace) immediately started building plywood replicas. "They were as close as they could get to our Malibu boards until the first load of balsa came in," Noll recalled, "and they couldn't make them fast enough."

For his part, Greg Noll came home with films of Australia, which in turn aroused American interest in the land Down Under. The cross-pollination between California and Hawaii was triangulated, and the timing was oddly providential. Almost at that precise moment, a salesman for Reichold Plastics walked into Hobie Alter's Dana Point surf shop with a sample of a new material for which his company was seeking applications. It was called polyurethane foam, and it would prove to be a supreme agent of change.

< Hobie and the Foam Revolution >

Hobie Alter was a California kid who grew up in Laguna Beach and found his great joy in the ocean waves. Almost no one was stand-up surfing there in those days, and Hobie was content with bellyboards and skimboards, until one day he borrowed an ultralight 30-pound fiberglassed-balsa surfboard from Walter Hoffman. Immediately, the 15-year-old Alter had to have one, Hoffman agreed to show him how to build his own Malibu chip.

Once Hobie had his balsa chip, the other kids on the beach just had to have one, too. So Hobie made 'em. He set up shop in his parents' front yard, charging materials and labor (about $20 per board). He averaged twenty boards a summer through high school and junior college. Then his dad kicked him out of the yard and into his own shop in Dana Point, a little town just down the road, where Hobie Surfboards opened in February 1954. "People I knew laughed at me for setting up a surf shop," Hobie recalled. "They said that once I'd sold a surfboard to each of the 250 surfers on the coast, I'd be out of business. But the orders just kept comin'."

With the stability, mobility, and financial security of the peacetime '50s, Americans were spending more time at the beach. Teenagers had gained tremendous independence, gas was cheap, and air travel was affordable. There were even a few surfers on the East Coast now, and occasionally Hobie shipped a board back there. By 1957, Hobie was bringing in extra shapers to help meet demand. He hired Phil Edwards, who was gaining a reputation as the best surfer in California, and Reynolds Yater, a supreme craftsman who would still be shaping the finest boards 40 years later.

A Reichold Plastics salesman showed up with his foam stuff at an especially critical juncture. Surfing

Originally surfboards were built on saw-horses on the beach or in garages, but by the late '50s some shapers were setting up shop, and by the early '60s, they were doing big business. Greg Noll's Hermosa Beach surf shop was state of the art in 1964. Left: Hobie Alter (left) with his star surfer and shaper, Phil Edwards, the first professional surfer. Hobie saw the future of foam and pioneered development of modern surfboard construction.

was growing fast, but the availability of wood wasn't. Competition for South American balsa was heating up, and then Dale Velzy moved his operation from the South Bay to San Clemente, just four miles from Dana Point. So Hobie began to test the new foam, trying to develop methods of blowing a uniform, strong, clean product that could be reliably shaped with a power planer. He moved one of his glassers, Gordon "Grubby" Clark, over to the foam-blowing project, and in 1958, they set up a foam shop in Laguna Canyon.

The salesman that visited Hobie didn't stop there; other shapers were working on the development of foam in the late '50s too, notably Dave Sweet, a brilliant surf-chemist who was a part of the Santa Monica scene. But Hobie was moving faster.

In 1959, Columbia Pictures released a film called *Gidget,* based on the 1957 novel by Frederick "Fritz"

Eugene Burdick's 1956 novel, The Ninth Wave, *preceded* Gidget *by a year, but a good first edition of* Gidget *was selling for $1,000 in the year 2000, while* The Ninth Wave, *by the author of* Fail Safe *and* The Ugly American, *was going for under $50.*

In the mid-'60s, a party at Greg Noll's factory brought the rival Orange County surf faction to the South Bay appropriately outfitted as the Dana Point Mafia. That's Mickey Muñoz in the sunglasses.

Kohner, who was fascinated with his daughter Kathy's real-life adventures on the beach at Malibu. The movie told a romantic tale of a free-spirited clan of rebel hedonists who lived, loved, and surfed on the beach, disdaining conventional society. Though thin of story, vaguely acted (it starred James Darren, with Sandra Dee as Gidget), and hopelessly saccharin, it hit the American youth audience right where it counted. Surf culture exploded into the mainstream.

"If that movie'd come out in the balsa era," Hobie said, "no one could have supplied 'em."

Where Waves Come From

Earth is the water planet. The polar caps are huge crystallized masses of it, the land is pocked and veined with it, and much, much more of it is buried underground. If you dig deep enough, this odorless, tasteless, transparent liquid is pretty much everywhere. And, of course, about 75 percent of the surface is covered with the stuff.

But it's no smooth sheet of glass out there. There's a lot of surface area—plenty of room to absorb the cosmic energy that stirs the upper atmosphere and migrates down to the surface in the form of wind, and that translates into the kind of wave action for which the sea is famous. The process of wave creation, like surfing, is simple but profound.

Ocean waves are generated by wind and storms: the friction of the atmosphere rubbing over the water surface literally pushes up ripples, which in turn are pushed into chop, which is pushed into larger seas, which organize themselves into bands of swell, which move relentlessly through the oceans (propelled, oddly enough, by gravity) until they strike land, releasing their stored cosmic energy as they break on the beaches that fringe the great seas of the world.

A perfect (but unsurfable) wave peeling over a shallow ridge of razor-sharp reef off Haapiti in Moorea. Above: Exploding surf on Pupukea reef during the big swells of December '69.

Malibu's Surfrider Beach in the summer of 1962. The empty waves of the '30s and '40s were a long way off.

The Boom Culture

< The Boom Culture >

"1956—Two black Cadillac limousines pull up at the pit on a full-bore hot summer's day in the era prior to total State control. In the limos sit the directors, leading players and author of the screen scenario *Gidget*. They are at Malibu to 'soak up atmosphere,' scout locations, and recruit surfing stand-ins and extras for the film. While the aliens stand on the beach and conspicuously attempt to keep the sand off their wing-tip shoes, several local boys gather bags of human excrement, and drop them into the mouths of the limousines' air-conditioning ducts. The cars leave, containing moguls and stars, travel about 300 yards, and stop abruptly while the cast and crew fall out of the cars and gag. Sandra Dee was reportedly observed vomiting on the center lane of the Coast Highway. Tubesteak figures if they hadn't needed air conditioning, it never would of happened."

—Craig Stecyk, "Malibu: Curse of the Chumash,"

Surfer Magazine, July 1976

At the close of the 1950s, the catalytic reaction seeded by surfing's pioneers was heading up the steep part of the growth curve. With the explosion in surfboard technology, surfing had reached critical mass at the beach. With its promise of freedom, near nudity, and excitement, the beach lured more and more kids from farther inland, and surfing was the handle they could grasp.

The first shops—Velzy & Jacobs, Hobie, Dave Sweet, the O'Neill Surf Shop up in San Francisco, then in Santa Cruz—got a sudden burst of competition from dozens of new builders. Reynolds Yater and Dick Perry were making boards

Propelled by the Hollywood film Gidget, *foam surfboards, and surf music, the surfing fad swept the USA in the early '60s. Texas, 1964: Enthusiasm and surfboards on the Padre Island seashore.*

70

at the Santa Barbara Surf Shop, Robertson-Sweet (Dave's brother) was advertising "surf now, pay later" in Pacific Palisades, Wardy was in Pasadena and Laguna Beach, Bob Olson was making Ole Surfboards in Sunset Beach, and Gordie was working in Huntington Beach.

But the explosion wasn't just a California phenomenon. In Florida, where the sport had been pioneered by Dudley and Bill Whitman in Miami (inspired by Tom Blake visits in the '20s and '30s) and Gauldin Reid in Daytona, Dick Catri and Jack Murphy were acrobatic divers in the late 1950s when Murphy picked up a Velzy & Jacobs balsa board. By the early '60s, under the moniker Murf the Surf Custom Surfboards, he was hawking products out of the Starlight Motel in Cocoa Beach, Florida, while growing numbers of surfers were putting pressure on local governments to gain access to the waves.

Surfing was also booming in Texas, where it had been introduced in the late '20s to Galveston beaches. "Doc" Dorian Paskowitz, legendary waterman Preston "Pete" Peterson, and the Columbo brothers caught the fever and spread the word in the 1930s. By the early '60s, Henry Fry had opened the Spring Branch Surf Shop in the Houston area, Mack Blaker was building boards near Galveston, George Hawn was busy in Port Aransas, and it was as if all of it had been made possible with the development of foam-and-fiberglass technology.

Meanwhile, foam of a different kind was making its impact as wetsuits extended surfing's range of places and seasons. Unlike latex rubber drysuits worn by Navy frogmen, neoprene wetsuits fit snugly, were flexible, and provided good insulation. Pioneered by Jack O'Neill in San Francisco and Santa Cruz and the Meistrell Brothers in L.A.'s South Bay area, the vests, jackets, and pants made of neoprene transformed surfing into a year-round sport in places like Northern California and the Pacific Northwest, the northeastern Atlantic States, England, France, and south Australia.

Right: Lance Carson's father watched Dale Velzy shape a board on the beach one day, then went home and carved a balsa blank into his son's first surfboard. By 1960, Lance was as good as any Malibu surfer had ever been. He integrated the fluid style of the "purist" school of surfing, a la Mickey Dora, with the complex maneuvers and nose-riding of guys like Dewey Weber. He was smooth and, in the best tradition of the best Malibu surfers, always a little surprising.

Lance Carson Surfboards

*Left: Surf fever caught hold of America's beaches. View from a Texas pier, c. 1960.
Below: Budding superstar Phil Edwards (left) with Ken Price and L. J. Richards at Trestles, mid-'50s.*

73

Da Cat

Miki Dora was surfing's Mohammed Ali. A guy who made a decisive lifestyle shift to follow his conscience into exile, he abandoned his fabled haunts to the Valley usurpers and Hollywood geeks. Here was a man of contradictions—a mumbler of sublime eloquence; a macho artist (a painter); a crude beach bum one minute, a debonair denizen of high society the next; a small-wave rider who proved himself at Waimea when there was honor (or money) at stake. His eloquent railing (often in print) against the forces of greed and growth became the sport's conscience. The only hope, he said, were the punks.

Dora's beach was Malibu, a small-wave spot, the classic hotdogger's wave—relatively fast but highly predictable, a perfect canvas for the artist surfers of Southern California to paint their
(cont'd on page 78)

< Malibu, Dora, and the Fall from Eden >

In 1960, the United States was in cultural transition: Eisenhower was retiring, Kennedy and Nixon were running for president, and the first American compact cars hit the market. Southern California had become the fastest-growing region of the country, and the arid earthquake zone was already famous for its tolerance of freaky fringe people. Culture met the sand in Santa Monica, home to a thousand surf legends.

The crowds at Malibu had thickened, and a long row of surfboards leaned against the barbed-wire fence that separated the beach from the Adamson house and the last vestiges of the gigantic Rindge rancho. A few steps from Pacific Coast Highway, an area of premium real estate known as "the pit" was the domain of the local elite—surfers who grew up riding these waves in the late '40s and the lazy '50s. They had explored the rudimentary performance tolerances of the Malibu chip boards, creating the stylized maneuvers, gestures, and poses of hotdog surfing. Now they saw their magic kingdom overrun with inland "kooks"—kids with little ability, no awareness of surfing's historical roots, and, hence, no membership in the sophisticated peer scene at the 'Bu.

Frankly, the local boys had gone a little sour on the whole thing. The pristine days on the California coast were gone, and quality of life was taking a big nosedive in direct proportion to the rise in population. By the time Cal Porter became Malibu's first lifeguard in 1959, there was anarchy in the air as the traditional hierarchy began to sag under the weight of hundreds of surfers. Matt Kivlin, a pioneer who had introduced a lot of young people to the waves of Malibu, rode his last wave there in 1962; he said it was too crowded.

The classic Malibu surfer of the 1950s was typically either a gung-ho gymnastic surf star in the mold of Lesley "Birdman" Williams or Dewey Weber, "the little man on wheels" (and former Buster Brown mascot and yo-yo champ), or the rebellious antihero typified by Gard Chapin and Matt Kivlin. Chasing and emulating these local heroes were the hot young kids—Mickey Muñoz, Kemp and Denny Aaberg, Bobby Patterson, the "Malibu Lizard" (Johnny Fain), and Lance Carson, who became one of Malibu's greatest on-the-water performing artists and perhaps the finest example of a "fusion" surfer, blending a soulful flowing style and physical subtlety with a knack for the full array of hotdog maneuvers. And then there was Miki "The Cat" Dora.

Miklos Szandor Dora II (a.k.a. Mickey Chapin, Miki Dora, Miklos S. Dora, MSD III, etc.) was truly a legend in his own time. Introduced to the surfer's life by his stepfather, Gard Chapin, the boy was a worthy student. Iconoclastic from the get-go, his early plan to fire-bomb the shack at San Onofre is just one example of the many outrageous scams, ruses, and poses that masked a man of extreme sensitivity and brilliance.

A sometime stunt double for several of the early '60s Hollywood beach flicks, Dora was known to push himself even beyond the limits of his own cool. "He was hired to do stunt riding in the movie *Ride the Wild Surf*. He wasn't a big-wave surfer, but they were paying him and he told them he could do it. The waves were really pumped up that day

Epitome of the bad-boy school of surfing, Mickey Dora assumed the stance of brilliant aquatic artist driven to bitter despair by the plundering of his pristine Malibu playground by hordes of inland zombies.

When he and Mickey Dora were fired as underwriters for Home Insurance Company (jobs they didn't hold long), Terry "Tubesteak" Tracey decided to become a full-time surfer instead. He collected palm fronds and driftwood and built this shack at Malibu, the epitome of cool and the center of gravity of the sub-culture celebrated in the 1957 novel Gidget.

Possession being nine-tenths of the law (and Malibu being his personal domain), Mickey Dora was famous for intentionally grounding kooks who dropped in on his waves. (Sequence) Dora "taps" an intruder. Below: In one of his final competitive appearances, Dora casually pushes Johnny Fain out of his way. Gestures such as this made him a cultural icon. Previous Spread: Mickey Dora (a.k.a. Miklos Szandor Dora) rides his wave at the 1965 Malibu Invitational surfing contest.

(cont'd from page 74)
stylish poses and maneuvers. A ride at Malibu could be an artistic meditation, a Zen experience far removed from the life-and-death tensions of surfing in the Hawaiian Islands. Southern California writer Dale Herd eloquently described Dora on such a wave in his 1970 opus on Miki Dora, "Superslicksurfcat and the Ethics of the Perfect Moment," in *Surfer:*

"This is Dora at his best, this time a motionless figure on a moving form, not just reacting cat-like to changes in the wave but actually controlling the wave by creating the entire line of action that you watch, this the entire and profound difference between the young yet skilled surfer, the athlete only, and the creative surfer, the artist."

Disillusioned with the "logjam" at his favorite surf spot, Dora bid farewell at the 1967 Malibu Invitational Surf Classic. There, competing for the last time, da Cat took off on a wave and trimmed beautifully across the blue-green wall until, passing in front of the judges, he bent over, dropped his black shorts, and mooned the gathered dignitaries and spectators.

at Waimea. He didn't like it . . . these were probably the biggest waves he had ever ridden in his life. That day, he had made a jump from five- or six-foot Malibu waves to twenty-foot Waimea. He was shaky, but he did it. The guy really had ability. I can't think of anyone else who could have made that sort of transition" (Noll and Gabbard, *Da Bull: Life Over the Edge*).

Taking his cues from the creative and pragmatic minds of Kivlin and Chapin, Dora saw the "new" surfing that he and a few others performed at Malibu in its peak years (say 1954–60) as fundamentally different than what had gone before. While by no means the only Malibu surfer resisting the tide of gremmies, kooks, and "Valley cowboys" who were invading Malibu's Garden of Eden, he nonetheless became the symbol of resistance.

A cult of localism, rooted as far back as the early days of Waikiki and the division of its beach into territories, became fashionable and flowered at Malibu. Every San Fernando Valley gremmie who came to Malibu had to slip through the narrow opening in the fence and pass the pit on the way to the surf. For many, passing this gauntlet was their first exposure to the rawest kind of profane insult and abuse. Their next exposure occurred when they paddled out and tried to catch a wave. Shouting down other surfers, behavior pioneered by Bob Simmons, now became a substitute for civil conversation. The street was moving off the beach and into the waves. A new social order was in the making.

Cast into surreality by the lens of Hollywood, the Malibu beach scene of the mid-'50s was the inspiration for a film genre and for a generation of insouciant poseurs. Frederick Kohner's novel about his daughter, Kathy (center), and her Malibu surfer friends (including "Tubesteak" in the white jacket, who was the inspiration for Kahoona) attracted thousands to the surf.

< Surf Nazis and Bushy, Bushy Blond Hairdos >

Mainstream media's portrayal of surfing has always been mixed. Articles in *Time* and other magazines in the late '50s and early '60s commonly debunked the surfing mystique, associating it with the unsavory world of bikers, hot-rodders, and drug addicts. It got pretty twisted with the addition of the word *Nazi* to the mix, which was reinforced by the surfers, of course—always on the edge of parody and satire, always with a kind of slapstick humor.

The surf nazi was incarnated for this editorial photo in Surfer. *In reality, no surfers would wear those helmets, except for pictures. Jim Fitzpatrick goose-steps to the nose at Malibu.*

The Nazi stuff started with the Pacific System Homes "Swastika" surfboards of the 1930s, which were popular on the coast. In the early '60s, there were Nazi skits in surf movies, swastikas on the Malibu wall and the Windansea pumphouse, and "Sieg heil!" stances out on the waves. And then Big Daddy Roth, described by *Time* magazine as "the supply sergeant for the Hell's Angels," created a line of fiberglass German-style "Surfer's Helmets." Roth's connection to the biker world manifested itself in the world's first plastic ghoul—"Surf Fink!"—produced and sold in the thousands (at least) by the Revell model company. Though it sported no swastika, it was certainly grotesque. Hollywood parlayed the biker associations in the Erik von Zipper subplots of the beach blanket movies.

The surf Nazi imagery aroused the ire of the general populace, many of whom already saw surfers as a bunch of "beach bums." In the mid-'60s, *Surfer* magazine railed against the use of Nazi associations, calling them "signs of the kook" (a kook being an unskilled surfer, or one with an "out of it" attitude), but the term *surf Nazi* has tenaciously remained a part of the subculture's vernacular, its meaning evolving to denote a hard-core surfer who focuses on surfing at the expense of other aspects of life.

Surfer wanted the public to see a kinder, gentler side of surfing—clean-cut kids wearing the uniform of Levi's, white T-shirts, and huarache sandals from Mexico, or baggies (long, loose Hawaiian-print surf trunks), bare feet, and peroxide-blond hair. It was just a good, clean, healthy sport. But, there was something quirky about surfin' on those waves out in California, and *Life* magazine seemed fascinated, running several articles characterizing surfers as goofy and stoked but not dangerous.

"Surfing, just beginning to catch on around the rest of the U.S., has become an established craze in California," proclaimed the magazine in an article titled "The Mad Happy Surfers" (September 1, 1961). "There are some 30,000 that revel in the delights of mounting their boards on waves hundreds of feet out and riding them in, feeling as though they could go on forever. The addicts are mostly teenagers for whom the sport, besides being healthy and immensely exhilarating, has become a cult."

There was no denying it. Surfing was a lifestyle that was starting to attract a curious interest from the heart of the country. It was a cult of addiction.

Right: "King of the Surf Guitar" Dick Dale and His Del-Tones, c. 1961.

Left: Two fantasies meet as Kathy Kohner and Sandra Dee compare notes on Moondoggie on the set of the film version of Gidget *in 1958.*

Bottom left: Gidget spawned an entire genre of Hollywood films, beginning with 1963's Beach Party, *starring Frankie Avalon and Mousketeer Annette Funicello (shown here), in which Mickey Dora made his motion picture debut as a beach boy.*

A Fender guitar classic, photographer Bob Perine shot this photo in June 1965 at Newport Beach. The surfer caught the first wave and rode in without getting a drop of water on the guitar.

< Hollywood and Vinyl >

"The movie *Gidget* was huge," wrote *Surfer* publisher Steve Pezman in 1977. "It swung surfing into mainstream prominence at a time when it was ready to accommodate new interest, thanks to foam, wetsuits, and accessibility."

The emergence of a mobile, rock 'n' roll–fired youth culture in the late '50s dovetailed perfectly with the subculture depicted in 1959's *Gidget*. Like 1954's *The Wild One* and 1955's *Rebel Without a Cause,* the film exposed an underground society of youth living by its own rules. But the film *Gidget* was a relatively tame piece of kitsch, with the only vaguely dangerous energy emitted by Cliff Robertson as Kahoona and a couple of the extras, who were real Malibu surfers. Mickey Muñoz, in a wig and bikini, doubled for Sandra Dee in the surf.

These films, all set in California, form a kind of evolutionary trilogy, and though the rebels blink in the last reel when Gidget and Moondoggie return to the establishment fold after their close brush with life's leading edge, significant cultural ground was laid on which a young generation would soon set up camp.

After *Gidget,* surfing endured almost a decade of caricature in Hollywood beach movies. There was *Gidget Goes Hawaiian* (1961), *Beach Party* (1963), *Muscle Beach Party* (1964), *Ride the Wild Surf* (1964), *Beach Ball* (1965), *Beach Blanket Bingo* (1965), and *Don't Make Waves* (1967). None captured anything remotely real about surfing or its culture, but the films worked at the box office, and every year there were thousands of new surfers buying boards and wetsuits.

If foam and bad films kicked off the surfing fad of the '60s, the real energizer was the new sound of surf music. Although music had been associated with surfing for a long time, in the past it had almost always been Hawaiian music. Many of the surfers and beach boys of California and Hawaii played music, and some worked in bands. Malibu surfers Tommy Zahn and Pete Peterson played with Ralph Kolsiana in Ralph's Beach Boys. Specializing in soft romantic Island tunes, the trio headlined at Sweeny's Tropicana in Culver City during the winter of 1953, but they never brought the house down the way Dick Dale did.

The "king of the surf guitar" and the father of surf music, Dick Dale and His Del-Tones emerged from out of the inland dust and smog of Riverside, California. Dale was so taken with the developing surfing scene—and surfing itself—that he took up the sport in the late '50s. He never got very good on a surfboard, but he could sure as hell wail on a fingerboard.

"Sometimes I'll look down at my strings," Dale once said, "and they have a black and blue tint to them from heating up." Playing left-handed with his guitar upside down (like Jimi Hendrix) and looking more biker than surfer, Dale thrilled audiences from Harmony Park in Garden Grove to the beautiful Rendezvous Ballroom on Balboa Peninsula. Already a legend in the rough by 1961, Dale and his band made their soundtrack debut in the film *Beach Party*. (Little Stevie Wonder made *his* debut in *Muscle Beach Party*.) Soon the halls and armories were rockin' with dozens of surf bands as the beach version of the sock-hop—the stomp—swept the coast and then the country.

"Surfing music was the first, and only, regional sub-genre of instrumental rock as well as the first time in pop history that a style of music grew out of, and around, a sport," wrote surf-band member John Blair in *The Illustrated Discography of Surf Music, 1959–1965*. "Simply stated, surf music was an attempt to express the feeling one received from riding the waves on a surfboard."

In the wake of Dick Dale's huge local success, a slew of bands sprang up in Southern California, too. They played Fender guitars with maximum reverb and had their band's name emblazoned on the bass drum. Two of these, the Surfaris and the Chantays, achieved national success in the early '60s, both with B sides of singles. The Surfaris, a high-school band from Glendora, recorded their first single, "Surfer Joe," with a B-side instrumental that was first titled "Stiletto" after a purchase in Tijuana. But the original opening—the flick of a blade—was too punk, and they decided to go with a surf name. Released with the title "Wipe Out," and opening with the snap of a piece of wood and manager Dave Smallin's shrill laugh, DJs preferred it to "Surfer Joe." The appeal was so great that the song was used as intro music on the British weekly pop show *Ready, Steady, Go,* and soon England's scooter-riding mods had adopted surf music as their own. Even Keith Moon, the drummer for the Who, was a bleached blond playing in an English surf band when the Who recruited him in the early '60s.

The Chantays were another band formed in a SoCal high school. Their 1962 "Move It" single was

Dick Dale's Surfer's Choice *launched a tsunami of surf music, then the Beach Boys took surfing to the American (and then international) mainstream, connecting a universal teenage angst with the specific and appealing imagery of California and the Pacific Coast beach scene.*

backed by a song first titled "Liberty's Whip," but changed to "Pipeline" after they saw a Bruce Brown surf movie featuring the famous wave. It was a good move in surf-mad 1963, and "Pipeline" rose to No. 4 on the Billboard charts. Even the Ventures, a band that was playing guitar instrumentals before the term *surf music* existed (and long after), covered the song. All over Southern California, bands adopted the surf sound.

Surfin' Safari *was the quintet's first big album, as Brian Wilson's lyrics gave voice to the oceanic rhythms launched by guitar virtuoso Dale (top, in the 1990s). Meanwhile from Balboa to Bondi, kids everywhere were doin' the surfer stomp.*

Hollywood was quick to sniff the popularity of surfing and offered up its own warped perspective on the culture in a series of camp and crazed productions.

While Dale and company defined the genre and suggested the lay of the land with their instrumental music, another musician was ensconced in his soon-to-be-famous "room" in Hawthorne, California, translating the poetry of surf for America's heartland. Brian Wilson was lead singer and lyricist for the Beach Boys, who originally called themselves The Pendletons (the most popular brand of cool-weather shirt among surfers). His brother Dennis was the only actual surfer in the group. The alienated moodiness of songs like "In My Room," the brokenhearted up-tempo pleas of "Help Me, Rhonda," and the weekend cruising bop of "Little Deuce Coupe" perfectly captured the mood of the times.

Along with Jan & Dean ("Little Old Lady from Pasadena," "Surf City," etc.), the Surfaris ("Wipe Out"), and a rash of new bands, the Beach Boys took elements of the surf sound and wove in stories of everyday life. A tribute to the power of their music was the way surf culture rode its swell farther and farther inland, as the euphoric glow of postwar America carried into the early '60s and, perhaps for the last time, pop music had a naïve quality that suggested life was great and everyone was having fun.

Even though there was no Surf City where there were "two girls for every boy," as Jan & Dean sang, it didn't matter. Surf music allowed people to vicariously share in the California dream. There was a spirit in surf music that anyone, anywhere could do it. New bands played songs about waves and surf spots while weathering the winters in midwestern cities. The most famous among these was Minneapolis' The Trashmen, who melded two existing songs, "Papa Oom Mow Mow" and "Bird's The Word," to form their own "Surfin' Bird." Even after they lost the copyright to the song in a legal battle, they released a full-length album titled *Surfin' Bird,* which featured a genuine cover of Dick Dale's "Miserlou."

Although the Beatles and the British Invasion of 1964 dealt a blow to the careers of the Beach Boys and other surf musicians, the imagery of surf music and the early surf movies continued to underpin and inspire surf culture. While surf music appeared to be dead, thousands of new surfers had been implanted with seductive images from the land of stoke.

< The Surf Media >

Drawn into the surfing boom and, in turn, feeding the building crescendo was a new generation of surf filmmakers, following the blueprint pioneered and proven by Bud Browne: shoot all winter, show all summer. Bruce Brown, John Severson, Greg MacGillivray, Jim Freeman, and others would create classics that have inspired generations of surfers. Even Greg Noll took more than a casual stab at a filmmaking career in the late '50s and early '60s, although he was never quite sure he was cut out for

Right: Surfer *magazine began as a 32-page booklet to be sold at John Severson's new surf film,* Surf Fever, *for $1.25.*

Left: Severson at the office, typing copy for The Surfer, *1959. No one was more responsible for creating popular surf culture than Severson, whose publication also stimulated an industry.*

Below: The Angry Sea *was a big hit for Severson in '63.*

JOHN SEVERSON
PRESENTS FEATURING SURF IN MEXICO, CALIFORNIA, AND HAWAII ■ PHOTOGRAPHED BY JOHN SEVERSON & RON CHURCH ■ IN COLOR ■ NARRATION BY JOHN SEVERSON
THE GREAT SURFING MOVIE OF 1963
THE ANGRY SEA
NEXT SHOWING
SPONSORED BY VAL SURF

this sort of thing. Noll ran the show, got their money, and got everyone out of there, but says it took 25 years off his life. "I wasn't that good on the technical aspects of those films," he admitted in a 1997 interview, "not like Severson and Bruce. I just basically loved surfing."

In 1957, backed and equipped by a flush Dale "World's Largest Manufacturer" Velzy, Bruce Brown set out to do a surf film that would promote Velzy's team riders. It was a prototypical journey that would become familiar as they surfed California, traveled to the Hawaiian Islands, drove in goofy beaters, and slept on the beaches. The resulting film, *Slippery When Wet,* was narrated live by Brown along with an offbeat Bud Shank soundtrack (stop talking, push the button, music, push the button, start talking). Bruce took the thing on the four-wall tour in 1958, just about the time the word *foam* was rising in surf consciousness.

While filming in Hawaii, Bruce encountered another young surfer, a cinematographer named John Severson, who was filming for his first surf flick, *Surf Fever,* which he toured in 1960. That same year, Bob Bagley brought around a film called *Sacrifice Surf,* and a guy named Bob Evans was touring Australia with a neat little surf-travel flick called *Surf Trek to Hawaii.* The star surfer in Evans' film was a young Aussie kid with a Phil Edwards style—Bernard "Midget" Farrelly. It was in 1961, when Columbia came out with *Gidget Goes Hawaiian,* that Evans countered whimsically with *Midget Goes Hawaiian,* the further adventures of Mr. Farrelly, who was quickly developing skill and confidence in the powerful Hawaiian surf.

The era of the single-lens reflex camera really hadn't dawned in the '50s. So when John Severson published his garage-built *First Annual Surf Photo Book* as a printed companion piece to his 1960 (cont'd on page 87)

Top: The Surfer *came first, and hundreds of others have followed. The emergence of the surfing magazines not only created a new marketplace, it synergized an audience and consolidated the subculture.*

Above: One of a score of young filmmakers who contributed to the stoke-a-thon of surf movies in the 1960s, Jim Freeman weighed in with his 1964 film Let There Be Surf.

As with Waimea, the day came when the impossible beckoned . . . and was achieved. It was appropriate that Phil Edwards, the acknowledged "best surfer in the world" at the time, be the first to surf the Banzai Pipeline in 1961. He named the spot after coming into the beach and exclaiming, "My God, it was perfectly dry in there!" Below: The July 18, 1966, edition of Sports Illustrated *featured Edwards on its cover with the blurb, "Surfing's East Coast Boom" and the caption, "Top stylist Phil Edwards rides at Virginia Beach."*

Phil Edwards: The First Professional

In 1955, the only surfer worth anything (beyond a lifeguard) was the guy who shaped your surfboard. But in 1963, when Hobie introduced the first signature model surfboard, Phil Edwards was the guy everyone said was the best in the world, and that was worth $23 for every board he shaped for Hobie.

Edwards was the supreme California power-surfing stylist. Thousands of kids saw him in Bruce Brown's *Surfing Hollow Days* and tried to emulate that genteel but infinitely assertive drop-knee backside turn, that ankle-to-ankle parallel stance in the slick throat of a glassy tube.

Edwards immortalized himself by being the first surfer to ride a wave at the notorious Banzai Pipeline. The photos that appeared in *Surfer* telegraphed the news around the world that the Pipeline had been conquered. No such announcement could have been made when Waimea was first ridden five years earlier. The existence of the magazines had changed everything. They created heroes, they shared stories, and they stoked the fever for surfing.

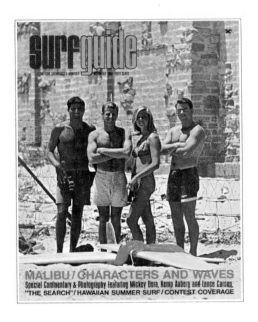

One of the first and best surf magazines was Surf Guide, *a direct competitor to* Surfer *for a couple of years. Late in the '60s, the Australian tabloid,* Tracks, *followed and achieved great success Down Under.*

movie, *Surf Fever,* many of the photos in its thirty-six horizontal pages were "frame grabs" from the 16mm film. Others were shot on location by Severson or his wife, Louise, "who manned the camera while I surfed." Titled *The Surfer,* the little book was a modest but exciting success—enough that Severson felt the market was ready for a quarterly. *The Surfer Quarterly* (later *Surfer Bi-Monthly* and, later still, simply *Surfer*) created and defined the surf magazine and, in doing so, an industry and a good measure of the sport itself. From 1960 to 1970, *Surfer's* per-issue press run went from 5,000 to more than 100,000.

Other surf magazines came and went. *Petersen's Surfing* ('63–'64) and *Surfing Illustrated* ('62–'67) were weak, never got better, and died. *Surf Guide* ('63–'65) was good, but its center of gravity was Malibu, while the epicenter of the emerging surf industry was in southern Orange County near Dana Point, where Severson had set up shop. As *Surf Guide* faded out of the scene, *International Surfing* faded in. A weak companion to *Surfer* throughout the '60s, it struggled for identity until the two reached some parity in the late 1970s.

Filmmaker Bob Evans brought surf publishing Down Under with *Australian Surfing World* (or simply *Surfing World*) in 1962. *The Australian Surfer* and *Surfabout* soon came on the scene, and all three were modeled on *The Surfer,* which was the rule until John Witzig came on the scene with *Surf,* one of the culture's most innovative publications. Witzig later joined in founding *Tracks,* which broke new ground in irreverent surf journalism.

These and a dozen more magazines and films amplified grassroots surf culture. They provided a non-mainstream layer of cultural context that had a huge impact on the development of surfing. Surfers in Hawaii or San Diego or Cape Hatteras could now see what surfers at Malibu or Santa Cruz were doing. They could see their boards, their maneuvers, their styles—who was hot and why—and what was possible.

When Santa Barbara knee-rider and innovator George Greenough built a fiberglass/Plexiglas water housing for his camera and took it under the curl of a wave to take a close-up shot of Australian Russell Hughes in the barrel in 1967, surf photography took an immediate leap forward. Other photographers took to the water, creating a dynamic alliance between the art, capitalism, and unique magic of a breaking wave. Surfers pulled out all the stops and went for their wildest moves. Everyone wanted to be in the magazines or in the movies.

< Advertising Catches the Wave >

In 1962, surfer and college student Duke Boyd recognized an emerging niche; he made a deal with a contract sewing operation in San Diego to build surf trunks for the growing legions of wave riders. He would model the trunks after those made by the legendary M. Nii, a Waianae, Oahu, tailor who made long ones with stripes down the side for the Makaha crew. Boyd named his new company after a state-of-the-art hotdog maneuver: Hang Ten. The logo: two bare footprints. An industry within an industry was thus born, and the child would soon outgrow the parent.

It didn't take long for Madison Avenue to catch on. The surf industry was on the rise, and as the chemistry of surfboard manufacturing got more complicated and the volume got higher, the need for more efficient working environments became apparent. Soon "surfboard factories" were occupying large areas in old buildings or industrial parks, and once they were up and running, with business scaled to large volumes, companies needed to maintain market share. Advertising was the solution, and it opened the door for a new job description: "professional surfer."

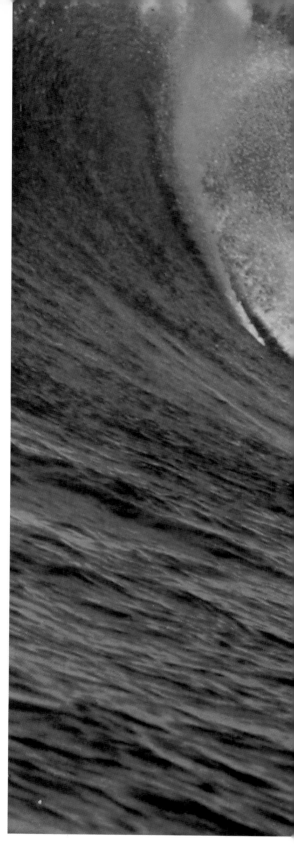

Although surfing had been depicted as a lifestyle tie-in by advertisers since the turn of the century (by cruise lines, beverage companies, etc.), Jantzen, a Portland, Oregon–based swimwear manufacturer, was the first mainstream player to directly target the surf market. The company contracted the back cover of *Surfer* in 1963 and was a fixture there for several years. Ironically, their first surf model was Pat Curren, a reclusive big-wave rider (tellingly, perhaps, he is looking out to sea, away from the camera, in the ad). Jantzen rotated a small stable of stars in its ads for trunks, jackets, and shirts, including Ricky Grigg ($2,000 a year), Corky Carroll ($1,500 a year for the most successful contest surfer of the '60s), Jerry West (of the L.A. Lakers), and even *Surfer* publisher Severson.

As the surf market grew, so did the industry, and by 1962 the sport had its own trade show—the Surf-O-Rama, held at the Santa Monica Civic Auditorium. Surfboard builders were experimenting with new manufacturing techniques to increase production and efficiency. Using molds, shaping machines, chopped-glass appliers, and other techniques, mass-produced surfboards ("pop-outs") began to appear on the market, and though no real surfer would be caught dead with one, many novices didn't know the difference. But the market was surprisingly sophisticated (thanks to the magazines), and the pop-out companies quickly failed. So did the intrepid soul who developed and marketed a motorized surfboard—one of several '60s gimmicks that were doomed to the trash heap (or the museum of curiosities) from the moment of invention.

Above: Corky Carroll and Sherri Haley in Keds ad, c. 1966. Notice the celebrated surf knots on Corky's knees, achieved through years of knee-paddling.

Right: Dr. Don James' thrilling image of Rusty Miller sliding down a Sunset Beach behemoth was purchased by the Hamm's Brewing Company and became perhaps the most-seen surfing image of all time, gracing billboards across America. That's Mickey Dora paddling out in the foreground and looking a little concerned about the approaching wall of water.

< Critical Mass on the North Shore >

Thanks to the 3 Ms (movies, music, and magazines), surfing was reaching critical mass on almost every shore. Hobie was selling more surfboards on the East Coast than anywhere else, and young surf stars from Florida were appearing on the scene—hot kids like Claude Codgen, Gary Propper, and Mike Tabeling. Propper's royalties from sales of his Hobie signature model made him the highest-paid surfer of the 1960s.

Where once the haole surfer was a relative rarity in Hawaii, now the beaches of Makaha and the North Shore were dominated by surfers from the mainland, mostly Californians. At times this made for ugly interracial tensions, and the stories of fights and "punch-outs" between haoles and *mokes* (a derogatory term for local Hawaiians) have become part of the lore of the pioneering years. Local tolerance for packs of half-naked and penniless surfers in their rusted cars, living ten to a shack and stealing coconuts and passion fruit to survive, was ebbing.

Nevertheless, with the Pipeline and Waimea barriers broken, the North Shore taboo began to erode, and more and more surfers, bringing ever-improving equipment, arrived to challenge the winter "heavies." Dave Rochlen (who built surfboards for Gary Cooper, among others, in California governor Earl Warren's garage) came over to Honolulu and established Surf Line Hawaii with partner Fred Schwartz. The first shop in the Islands to offer multiple mainland surfboard brands, along with repairs and rentals, Surf Line created an industry presence in Hawaii. Soon, several other shops opened their doors in Honolulu and elsewhere in Hawaii, and the manufacturing of the most contemporary kind of equipment returned to the source.

A cottage industry began to spring up on the North Shore, too. The fragile foam-and-glass boards were vulnerable in the powerful Hawaiian surf. There was a need to repair or replace dinged or broken boards. By the mid-'60s, in carports and sheds along the North Shore, surfboards—especially "big guns"—were being made precisely to ride the winter waves.

The major big-wave spots became quite the circuses by the mid-'60s. With film crews and photographers on the beach (and soon out in the water), the number of surfers looking for the power and the glory was on the rise. Out in the "country," visiting surfers and mainland transplants (like Fred Van Dyke, Ricky Grigg, Peter Cole, Buzzy Trent, Butch Van Artsdalen, Jose Angel, and a hundred others) met and blended at a dozen major spots with ever-increasing numbers of young local surfers (like Barry Kanaiaupuni, Eddie and Clyde Aikau, Tiger Espere, Jock Sutherland, and Joey Cabell). As the numbers grew and the local economy began to consider surfers as a resource, the buzz got out that the North Shore was happening. When large numbers of spectators began to turn up for the winter action (many of them young women attracted by the hard-bodied surfers, or to surf), it was only a matter of time before broader media interest followed.

Greg Noll contemplates the shorebreak at Banzai Pipeline. On this day in 1964, he paddled out to Third Reef Pipeline and, after hours of waiting for the right moment, paddled into one of the largest waves ever attempted. As he rode across the mighty wall, the water was being sucked up the face faster than he could surf down it, and he suffered a horrific wipeout. Noll continued to push the big-wave envelope until 1969, when he took off on the largest wave ever ridden at Makaha.

The Surfer

The surfer is a strange sort of amphibious creature, a throwback to an ancient past, a messenger from a distant and future world. A practitioner of an activity born long ago in remote Pacific islands, the surfer has always marched to a different drummer, certainly a different drummer than historic European culture.

Surfers are tuned to the rhythm of the tides and the cycling onslaughts of storm and swell. To surf with enough regularity to be proficient (and surfing's more fun if you're good at it), you must be able to arrange your life to be where the surf is happening. And when it's happening—when the swell is there and conditions are good—you want a piece of it. So you live with a dual awareness, an acquired extra consciousness that's constantly monitoring the situation, waiting for the call. "Hey, this is Ed. The point is perfect, let's hit it!" Surfers are always ready to turn on a dime.

Right: To surf is to travel, so the surfer is a nomad. Surfer and "The Beast" at Velzyland, c. 1962.

Above: The beach was totally inundated by the last set of waves as this surfer cautiously considers paddling out before the next. Waimea Bay, December 1977.

For several years prior to the 1966 World Contest in San Diego, noseriding was the most respected and admired maneuver in surfing. As a result, David Nuuhiwa (in full nose-arch, top) became the sport's most respected and admired surfer. Inset: David on the beach at Oceanside during the 1972 World Contest after the switch to shortboards. The most successful competition surfer of the 1960s was Corky Carroll (below), shown at Poche testing the Hobie noserider that won the 1965 Tom Morey Invitational, a noseriding contest offering cash prizes.

< Toes on the Nose and David Nuuhiwa >

Standing on the nose of a surfboard, even putting the toes of one or both feet over the tip of the board ("hanging five" and "hanging ten," respectively), is one of the most difficult maneuvers in surfing, and in 1964, that single maneuver in all of its variations had captured the attention and affection of nearly every surfer on the planet. Noseriding, as it was termed, was God, and the best noserider in the world was a skinny Ala Moana (Honolulu) surfer named David Nuuhiwa.

Shock waves rippled through the California surf scene when Nuuhiwa moved to the mainland in the early '60s. The kid's ability to stand on the nose, seemingly for minutes (actually up to ten to twenty seconds), convinced the top surfers that they were suddenly being overtaken on the evolutionary ladder. "David arrived on the coast, and immediately occupied center stage," recalls surf historian Craig Stecyk. "Nuuhiwa's precociousness ushered in the era of high-performance noseriding."

Noseriding was such a clear act of ability, such a public demonstration of surfing prowess that was so easy to understand, it almost became synonymous with surfing. "You're a surfer? Can you hang ten?" That was it: ten toes over the nose. Hanging five was fine, but if the back foot was too far back, they called it a "cheater five."

David Nuuhiwa didn't introduce hanging ten to the mainland—surfers at Malibu had been doing it for years. But David (he was always called "David," as if there was no other, so large was his "mysto" factor) made noseriding an art form.

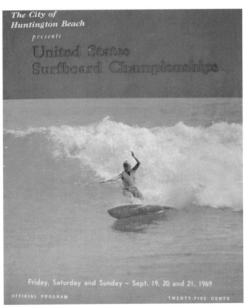

The first post-war contest of magnitude on the West Coast was the United States Surfing Championship at the Huntington Beach pier, an annual event begun in 1959. The 1969 edition (program above) featured Hawaiian Reno Abellira (right) in the requisite helmet with his Dick Brewer–designed surfboard with its hyper-kicked nose.

< Surfing Goes Competitive >

Competition has always played a role in surf culture. In ancient Hawaii, chickens, canoes, wives, and lives were all fair game when the surf was up and the betting began. Revived in Waikiki early in the twentieth century, surfing contests emphasized paddling competition, sometimes over distances of ten or twenty miles. At that time, riding waves was seen more as an expressive rather than measurable activity, but in the California surf club championships in the 1930s, wave riding began to be seen as a central competitive discipline. Surf clubs—from the Outrigger and the Hui Nalu in '20s Waikiki, to the Palos Verdes and Long Beach surf clubs of the '30s–'50s, and to the Windansea and Malibu clubs of the '60s—provided the context and incentive for competition, and most modern surf contests prior to the mid-'60s were between surf clubs.

The most notable exception was the annual Makaha International Surfing Championships, first held in 1952. While paddling dominated the first two years of the event, good waves materialized for the January 1954 running, and champion paddler and hot-curl stylist George Downing (riding a new high-performance finned surfboard) won the event in spectacular style. Surfing became the headliner of the event, which in turn became the model of surf competitions worldwide.

Although vaguely antithetical to a subculture that was otherwise notoriously "hang-loose," structured competition grounded in interclub rivalries in the U.S. and Australia began to flourish. The better surfers of the '60s emerged out of these organizations and the competitions between them—Mike Doyle, Skip Frye, Ricky Irons, Rusty Miller, Corky Carroll, Mark Martinson, Steve Bigler, David Nuuhiwa, Mike Purpus, and a hundred other "name" surfers—earned their reputations in contests.

The first surfing contest to offer significant prize money was the Tom Morey Invitational ("25 surfers noseriding for $1500.00") in Ventura, California, over the 1965 Fourth of July weekend. The rules were simple: The winner would be the one who accumulated the most time standing on the front 25 percent of the surfboard in fourteen rides. Mickey Muñoz won by seven-tenths of a second (by a judging error; San Diego's Mike Hynson actually won), and the event caused quite a stir.

The Morey Invitational not only stimulated noseriding as a technique, it goosed design thinking in a way the sport hadn't seen since Dale Velzy went off in a paroxysm of weird experimentation (Bump, Pig, 7-11, et al.) in the late '50s. Muñoz's winning board was shaped by Phil Edwards at Hobie. A wide board with a concave scoop under its nose, its success led to a flurry of noserider models, which dominated the mainland surfboard market for the next few years. Surfboard shops reaped the windfall as demand for new and different brought a fresh cycle of fashion (and obsolescence) to the sport. Contest creator Morey—part mad scientist, part dream merchant, and part surfer—would go on to create the Boogie Board™, the short, square-nosed, soft-foam bellyboard that would one day be used by millions of people worldwide.

95

On any day of the year it's summer somewhere in the world. Bruce Brown's latest color film highlights the adventures of two young American surfers, Robert August and Mike Hynson who follow this everlasting summer around the world. Their unique expedition takes them to Senegal, Ghana, Nigeria, South Africa, Australia, New Zealand, Tahiti, Hawaii and California. Share their experiences as they search the world for that perfect wave which may be forming just over the next Horizon. **BRUCE BROWN FILMS**

Into Africa: Robert August, Terrence, Mike Hynson, Jack Wilson, Bruce Brown, and Max Wetland on the scent of the perfect wave near Cape St. Francis. The Endless Summer *poster was designed by former* Surf Guide *and* Surfer *art director John Van Hamersveld.*

The Endless Summer

Bruce Brown began surfing circa 1950 in the Huntington Pier–Seal Beach area. After high school, he joined the navy to escape the draft and went to submarine school in Connecticut. "I'd read an article in *Reader's Digest* that if you went to sub school and got in the top ten percent of your class, you could choose your coast, and the top guy could choose his submarine." Brown finished at the top of his class, chose Pearl Harbor, and then picked duty that kept him on the island so he could surf.

"The first night I went down to Waikiki, got a newspaper and slept on the beach under the newspaper," he recalls. "I thought it was just amazing. I'd seen pictures of Hawaii and one of Bud Browne's movies, but being there was something else!"

In 1963, Bruce was back in Hawaii, this time working on a new film. The theme wouldn't be that different from his last one, *Surfing Hollow Days,* just a little more focused: Two surfers, Mike Hynson and Robert August, hitting the road to follow the summer and the surf around the world. Brown and crew filmed in Senegal, Ghana, Nigeria, South Africa, Australia, New Zealand, Tahiti, Hawaii, and California. Things didn't

always go the way they planned, but then Bruce Brown wasn't the kind of person to do that much planning anyway. He was more in the "school of flow." Somehow, even when they had no luck with the surf, something would happen. They'd meet someone; there'd be something to do. It was cinema verité, and everything seemed just perfect, especially the wave they came upon at Cape St. Francis in South Africa. In that sequence, Brown found his magic. When the film was finished, he knew he had something good in the can.

Brown had a new man working with him when the film hit the four-wall circuit in 1964. Paul Allen, a surfer, had come into the office one day and said he wanted to help Bruce promote his films. "He said, 'Don't pay me. If I make you money, I'll get something,'" Brown recalls. "It's a little hard to turn that kind of a deal down. And he was real good at it."

With Allen arranging the shows and coordinating publicity, *The Endless Summer* was a big success on the circuit—so big that Brown and Allen decided to look for a national distributor. With Brown's easy homespun narration woven into a nice soundtrack by the Sandals, they went to work trying to sell it. Hoping a successful run in the U.S. heartland would be convincing (if it worked), they booked a theater in Wichita, Kansas,

then the obscure Kuyps Bay Theater in New York City. After breaking records in both houses and pleasing the critics, they attracted a distributor. The rest is history.

When the film went into distribution in 1966, audience reaction was similar to the crowds on the beaches of Senegal and Ghana when Robert and Mike had paddled out and started riding waves right in front of their villages—they were stoked! Brown, too, was stoked—his $50,000 investment brought him millions.

What was the film's special attraction? "I don't know," Bruce Brown admits. "I've run into so many people who saw *The Endless Summer,* particularly back East, and said it had some effect on them. But a lot of 'em, they didn't surf, and they never *did* surf. It's always been a mystery to me."

It may have been a mystery, but a lot of people related to it. At a time when the national anthem was "Let's go surfin'!" a major irony had come to a head: surfers, the core culture of escape, were feeling in serious need of escape. Besides, the magazines and films had revealed a world of untapped waves. Brown's film had crystallized a vision of a new grail and the next phase in surfing—adventure travel—and *The Endless Summer* instantly became the central vision of surfing.

96

< The First World Contests >

When the crew of *The Endless Summer* flew in from South Africa, they learned too late that the best waves in Australia come in the winter. But they arrived in time for a summer of small waves and new friends, notably a kid named Robert Young. Nicknamed "The Gnat," Young was a rising star from the North Sydney beaches and the new Australian junior champion. He had a brash naturalness and a strong presence, so Brown worked him into the film.

They also encountered an old friend from Hawaii, Bernard "Midget" Farrelly, who was already the most famous surfer in Australia. Cinematographer and publisher Bob Evans had been quick to pick up on Midget's extraordinary surfing ability, boyish innocence, and agreeable disposition, and made him the star surfer of several of his films and the subject of regular magazine articles. When Young displaced Farrelly at the top of the competitive and cultural pyramid in the mid-'60s, a rift developed between the two that never healed (they even wrote competing surfing columns in the Sydney newspapers), yet their similarities could be as strong as their differences (for instance, both emulated Phil Edwards).

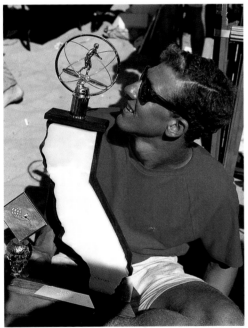

Although they dominated media attention, Farrelly and Young were not only the preeminent surfers to come out of Australia in the '60s. Knowing that the inherent coastal orientation of Australia made it a surfer's paradise, and that the Aussie kids—not just Young and Farrelly—were damn good, Bob Evans personally conceived and engineered the first World Surfing Championship, which was held in 1964 at Manly, near Sydney. Remarkably, the contest attracted the best surfers from Hawaii and California as well as Peru, Great Britain, and other countries. Huge crowds swarmed the broad beach and bluffside at Manly (not far from Freshwater), and the championship was a great success. Not surprisingly, in less-than-unanimous judging, Farrelly was the popular winner and became the sport's first world champion.

Some of the best American surfers stayed after the contest to travel and surf in Australia, notably Hawaii's Joey Cabell (who some said should have won the Manly event). A surfer of extraordinary gifts, Cabell surfed with a poised style and a penchant for speed that earned him his nickname, "The Gazelle." Cabell's surfari up the coast to Angourie and other spots opened his eyes to the quality of Aussie surf, and his surfing opened the eyes of the Australians to what was possible on their own waves. In the wake of Evans' world contest, the popularity and the quality of surfing in Australia took another leap forward.

Duke Kahanamoku brought Waikiki saltwater to San Diego for the '66 World Contest; here (top) he consecrates the event at Ocean Beach. The Olympic swimming champion and Father of Modern Surfing died the following year. A statue at Waikiki commemorates his life. Above: Australian iconoclast Nat Young with the '66 trophy.

Although it initiated a process that led to a series of World Contests (Peru in '65, San Diego in '66, Puerto Rico in '68, Australia again in '70, and San Diego again in '72), Evans' Australian event was never recognized by the International Surfing Federation (a self-appointed Peru-Hawaii-California organizing committee). The first official World Contest was held the following year in Peru, and it was won by Peruvian Felipe Pomar, the first official world surfing champion.

The Peruvians had discovered surfing back in the '50s when an airplane pilot spotted beautiful surf breaking far below and notified his friend George Downing back in Hawaii. The spot, which broke something like Makaha, was named Kon Tiki and was first legitimately surfed by Downing on a balsa board in 1955. The surf is consistent if not pristine in Peru. A group of wealthy Peruvians established a surf club at Miraflores called the Waikiki Beach Club, and the country fielded teams for the big international contests.

Worlds collided at the 1966 World Contest in San Diego. The victories of Farrelly and Pomar seemed to indicate it was California's turn, and it was fully expected that David Nuuhiwa and his ten-second noserides would carry the day. But Australian Nat Young came to the hotbed of surf culture with a magic surfboard he called "Sam" and proceeded to demolish the opposition with a demonstration of powerful, no-frills surfing that embarrassed the Californians and shocked them out of their hang-ten reveries.

Young's victory over Nuuhiwa, Corky Carroll, Jock Sutherland, Mike Hynson, and the rest of the hot-dogging surf stars ushered in a period of confusion, nationalism, and defensiveness, as the California "hot performers" tried to minimize what had happened at the hands of the Aussie "total involvement" philosophy, which rejected California-style surfing's exaggerated poses and gimmicky surfboard designs. The lads from Down Under had a new, George Greenough–inspired vision of what surfing was, and it was revolutionary in its simplicity: Set your mind free!

< Surf Travel >

The first surfers—the Polynesians—were bold travelers, and the twentieth-century migrations of surfers to Hawaii primed the modern era for travel. Southern California surfers' discovery of nearby Baja opened the doors to new adventures and discoveries. It was always great to find a new spot, surf virgin waves, and maybe even dare a taste of the forbidden—such as an evening of drunken debauchery at the Blue Fox in Tijuana. But it was the epiphany of Cape St. Francis—that perfect, peeling wave waiting at the end of a long trek over the dunes in *The Endless Summer*—that ignited the explosion in surf travel that would shape the sport for the rest of the millennium.

Ironically, while traveling surfers were discovering new places to surf, the citizens of those places discovered surfing. By the mid-'60s, traveling surfers (many of them filmmakers looking for ever more exotic waves) had spawned cultural outposts around the world— Peru, England, Puerto Rico, New Zealand, Japan, South Africa, and France (pioneered by the writer Peter Viertel while on the Basque coast for the shooting of his script of Hemingway's *The Sun Also Rises;* his wife, actress Deborah Kerr, became the patroness of the first French surf club, Waikiki). Each outpost was not only a destination, but a jumping-off point for further exploration. A silent network of prototypical travelers was always out there working the edges, riding new waves in places no one back home had ever even heard of. Soon they would report back, and the travel fever would be stoked even further.

The essence of surfing is grace under pressure. Joey Cabell epitomized the concept during the 1968 Peruvian International Surfing Championships, when he entered the ring for the first time and knew exactly how to face the bull . . . in surfer style.

An early prototype of the traveling surfer was Peter Troy, a self-described adventuring amateur anthropologist, who set out from his native Australia in 1963 to explore the world for perfect waves and personal freedom. "It's very simple," he told *Surfer* in 1968, "I'm devoted to surfing, and while I'm traveling, I like to evaluate human life, especially in its primitive form." On his 125,000-mile odyssey, Troy won the first European surfing championship in 1963, a small-wave contest in Peru in '64, was barred from Syria after attempting to smuggle in kosher Mexican jumping beans, and was the first person to surf in Ceylon, Italy, Gibraltar, the Canary Islands, Ecuador, Argentina, Panama, and a dozen other countries.

98

Nat Young and the Involvement School

"I first met Nat in Sydney," recalls McTavish. "He was living at Collaroy, and I was shaping at Scott Dillon's factory in '62. Nat was just a raw kid—gangly, but with incredible talent. He was mimicking Midget for the first couple of years, and Midget was mimicking Phil Edwards, but I had no doubt that some day Nat would rise over that and become his own man, and then he'd be incredible."

At a chance encounter with Nat at a Sydney-area surf contest one day, McTavish laid out the facts of life. "If there's two trains on the same track," he said, "one can never over-take the other. But if you change tracks, you can roar off at your own speed." Nat took the counsel seriously, breaking away, shedding Edwards, Farrelly, and McTavish in one fell shift of attitude and opening the doors of the "involvement" school of surfing in Australia. "With his move into the involvement school of thinking in '65–'66, Nat become liberated . . . and that was on long boards!" says McTavish.

The involvement school of surfing rejected the entire circus-like paradigm of California-style surfing with its noserides and hotdog maneuvers. "It was a very functional approach," says McTavish, "making maximum use of the waves, staying close to the curl, being, I guess, pure. No dress-up. Form follows function. . . . Boiled down to the basics: You rode waves hard and

When the Australians met Dick Brewer and his test pilots in Lahaina, the cross-pollination was achieved and the shortboard idea became a full-blown revolution in equipment and wave-riding style. Nat Young in a particularly seminal moment at Honolua Bay on Maui.

deep and steep, and how you looked was a by-product."

Nat Young embodied this new approach to surfing, and his personal style was a mirror to his approach in the water. The second great Australian surfer to emerge under Bob Evans' tutelage, Young was an aggressive, sometimes ruthless competitor who went through enormous personal changes during the so-called psychedelic era.

99

< Plastic Machines and the Shortboard Revolution >

In the aftermath of the World Contest, while Australian surfer and journalist John Witzig proclaimed "We're Tops Now!" in the May 1967 edition of *Surfer* and the Yanks worked on damage control, Nat was back in Australia, where he found that things had already changed. Suddenly his own 9-foot-4-inch board (which he'd left back in California to be admired) was as obsolete as the noseriders it had vanquished. *Short* was the operative word now. "When [Nat] came back, he spent a period of fame as the world champion, being feted around the city," recalls Bob McTavish, who had inspired Nat's surfboard design. But when he came north again, "he got a shock to see that we'd suddenly discovered shortboards, and he rapidly tried to catch up, and he did. He caught up and overtook all the Australians. By late '67 he was looking pretty amazing."

Young dropped out of sight and into the creative kitchen that was brewing new ideas up the coast in Byron Bay. What emerged were short, wide-tailed boards with vee-shaped bottoms and deep, flexible Greenough-style fins. The boards were 8 feet six inches and getting shorter by the week. When

Bob McTavish, architect and primary test pilot of the vee-bottom and early short-board designs, led the paradigm shift from Australia to California. He followed George Greenough to the Santa Barbara coast in 1967 and experimented on secluded Channel Islands waves, where Greenough captured him carving this radical backside turn.

Witzig looked at McTavish's latest and exclaimed, "It looks like a plastic machine!" the name stuck. In exquisite synchronicity, a hot new goofy-foot kid from Victoria, Wayne Lynch, got involved and single-handedly redefined the lines that could be drawn on the face of a wave. It was an exciting and explosive time, and it really seemed like anything *was* possible.

About this time, California's prestigious Windansea Surf Club paid a visit to Australia to compete in a post–World Contest showdown. Documenting the trip was a young man named Eric Blum, an associate producer with Twentieth Century Fox who hoped to make "a truly professional film on the sport." Whatever Blum's movie was going to be called, it became *The Fantastic Plastic Machine,* virtually ignoring the Windansea team, as Young, McTavish, and Greenough captivated the filmmaker's attention. "Nat was the first surfer I had ever met whose ideas matched his incredible surfing skills," gushed Blum. While it never achieved wide distribution, *The Fantastic Plastic Machine* clearly illustrated the shortboard paradigm shift: It wasn't simply a change in equipment that was sweeping through surfing, it was a change of consciousness.

McTavish was one of twenty-four of the world's best big-wave surfers invited to the prestigious 1967 Duke Kahanamoku Invitational (the contest was established in 1965 as an alternative to the increasingly political Makaha International). When he arrived carrying a 9-foot, wide-tailed, vee-bottom Plastic Machine, no one knew what to think. Although he had problems with the board on the hollow, powerful, ten-foot Sunset waves, he soon joined fellow Aussies Young, Lynch, and Ted Spencer on a trek to Maui with John Witzig and his cinematographer brother, Paul. Their timing was good, and they encountered perfect waves at Honolua Bay. The resulting photos of Young and McTavish, showing a new style of surfing on the new boards, appeared in *Surfer,* and Paul Witzig's film, *The Hot Generation,* soon followed with a dramatic closing sequence of the vee-bottoms at Honolua Bay. The combo kicked the revolution into high gear.

What the surfboard industry initially resisted (trying hard not to have to eat its inventory of longboards) now began to pay off as it became clear that virtually every surfer in the world was suddenly in the market for a new board; one by one, all of the manufacturers got behind the shortboard program. But the industry seemed to be changing, as if a great democratization had occurred.

"The so-called underground guru surfboard builders are, in reality, the workers from the major surfboard firms going into business for themselves," stated veteran shaper Dick Brewer in a 1970 interview. "There are now a thousand surfboard shops where there used to be a hundred. The surfboard industry is in better shape than ever before; it's just that all the business is no longer in the hands of a few."

George Greenough's dished-out "spoon" kneeboards with blue-fin tuna-style fins and flexible tails caught the attention of the key Australian surfers and inspired the shortboard revolution.

< The George Greenough Influence >

Aftermath the 1966 World Contest, a seasonal visitor from California began to have an impact on Australian surfing. George Greenough was a surfer of a different sort. He surfed on his belly or his knees, riding a canvas air mattress or a short, scooped-out fiberglass kneeboard with a flexible tail and a deep foiled fin that he'd modeled after a bluefin tuna's. Already a living legend on the California coast, he was known for driving his gutted black-and-white Highway Patrol cruiser to obscure surf spots in search of uncrowded waves. A quasi-loner who was surprisingly loquacious when prompted to discuss his ideas, experiences, and technical theories, Greenough was the primary inspiration for the shortboard revolution of 1966–67.

Instead of an endless summer, George pursued endless winter, dividing his year between the

George Greenough's performances at Lennox Head, Australia (here in 1967) were the stuff of immediate legend. His short, flexible kneeboard carved revolutionary, tight lines on the hollow waves, inciting impressionable Aussies to cut two feet off their standard surfboards.

hemispheres, enjoying endless winter power and uncrowded conditions. His unique approach to surfing quickly attracted the attention of the surfers and shapers on the Central Coast north of Sydney. Bob McTavish was most impressed by Greenough's fins and began to adapt some of his "neutral-handling" high-performance ideas into regular surfboards. When the new Australian champion Nat Young visited McTavish while preparing for the 1966 World Contest, he met Greenough and was deeply impressed.

It was Greenough's 4-foot-10-inch, 6-pound, spoon-shaped kneeboard (nicknamed *Velo*) with its deep, elegantly foiled fin that inspired McTavish's designs at the time. And it was McTavish, as architect of the revolution, who translated those concepts into surfboards that led directly to "Sam," Nat's unusually thin 9-foot-4-inch Gordon Woods–manufactured surfboard (with a Greenough fin) on which he won the world title. Young's victory would send a shock wave through surfing and completely alter its course. In 1967, McTavish and his test pilots whacked another foot off their boards, introducing the radical vee-bottom design that ignited the world shortboard revolution.

< Into the Mystic >

In 1968, surfing experienced the greatest cultural and conceptual shift in its history as virtually the entire sport threw away its 9- and 10-foot boards and took up shortboards. In a single year, the sport was almost completely transformed. Surfboards went from 9 feet 6 inches to 8 feet 6 inches to 7 feet and below, and anyone on a longboard was surfing a dinosaur. The healthy, clean-cut look that had been carefully nurtured by a surfboard manufacturing industry interested in attracting new buyers collapsed in an explosion of long hair, beads, and funny-smelling smoke. Psychedelic imagery flooded into magazines, and surfing's latent pantheistic origins bubbled to the surface in ad copy like, "There's a divinity that shares our ends, Rough-hew them tho' we may . . . " (Rick Surfboards); "Karma: One's way of life is spirited from within . . ." (Bing Surfboards); and "From the Green House to the Green Room: Jacobs Surfboards are inspired by the green glory of the natural world."

The veil was thin, the shell had cracked, and surfers could talk to each other with new openness, even in ad copy. "Surfboards are not things to be ridden, but forms that will let you drive to the bottom, bury an edge, see a pocket and throw your mind at it," wrote Nat Young in a 1968 ad for Dewey Weber Surfboards. "I have aligned myself with Weber to give direction to my thoughts and experience. Some people have done it with music like Mike Bloomfield, John Mayall, and Eric Clapton. What they give you through their music is basic honesty. I can only give you this through surfing and my communication with you."

The door was flung open and new winds were blowing through. Out on the water, there was talk and conversation. Surfers encouraged each other, hooted for the other guy's good rides, talked board design and new possibilities. The virtual monopoly of a handful of surfboard manufacturers had been supplanted by a grassroots network of underground shapers working one-on-one with their customers, building boards in garages and small shaping rooms within blocks of every good surf spot known to man. The time for mass-production and pop-outs was over, and any manufacturer who wanted to stay in business needed to sign up "radical" and creative team riders to maintain market share.

Nat Young, the consummate surfer, completely in sync at Haleiwa in December '98. Note the refinement in surfboards that had occurred in just a year (see photo page 99).

Rick Griffin helped paint the psychedelic bus Motorskill for John Severson's Pacific Vibrations *in 1970, then returned to the coast north of San Francisco to explore new regions of art and consciousness. He was killed on April 16, 1991, when his Harley Heritage Softail motorcycle struck a left-turning delivery van. Above: Rick at Rights and Lefts on the Hollister Ranch near Point Conception.*

Rick Griffin

The shortboard revolution coincided with an enormous cultural change. Rick Griffin, the California artist who began by illustrating Greg Noll's *Surfer's Annual,* then moved to John Severson's *Surfer,* where he developed the lovable little surf gremmie he called Murphy, was soon producing spectacular psychedelic posters for the Grateful Dead, Jefferson Airplane, and Big Brother and the Holding Company. By the late '60s, Murphy was surfing through time and other dimensions, wearing the transcendent helmet of an ancient Hopi demigod and speaking in tongues.

"Rick really gave surfing a good image for a lot of people who really didn't think much of surfing," says Severson. "He took it out to New York and San Francisco." Griffin's work (as well as Severson's and several other surf-artists') was featured in a mid-'60s "sport and art" feature in *Sports Illustrated*.

After many personal transitions (including born-again Christian), Rick went down on his Harley Heritage Softail in August of 1991. "Rick, like the rest of us, was on a mission to turn on the world," said Jerry Garcia, not long before his own death in 1995.

The era of signature models morphed into the era of intimate soul-brother vibrational alignment. You rode what felt good, what let you express yourself. Flower power came to the beach.

Reflecting all these changes, a fusillade of imaginative, idealistic, and sometimes even well-made surfing films appeared in the late '60s and early '70s, most propelled by the psychedelic soundtrack of the time, which barraged surfing audiences with stoked paeans to organic bliss and tubular escape. Paul Witzig's *Evolution,* featuring the mind-altering surfing of the period's most imaginative surfer, Wayne Lynch, was probably the best example, but Hal Jepson's *The Cosmic Children,* George Greenough's *The Innermost Limits of Pure Fun,* John Severson's *Pacific Vibrations,* Fred Windisch's *The Natural Art,* Mastalka-French's *Seadreams,* MacGillivray-Freeman's *Waves of Change* and *Five Summer Stories,* Alby Falzon's *Morning of the Earth,* and Witzig's *Sea of Joy* were each revolutionary classics in their own way. Harmony with nature, surfing as art, and surfing as a tribal brotherhood were strong currents running through each of these films. As in the culture at large, there was great optimism afoot in surfing. Things had changed with the shortboard, the music, and the psychedelic drugs, and surfing would never be the same again.

< Dick Brewer and the Pocket Rocket >

As word got out that George Greenough and Bob McTavish were experimenting with new shortboard design ideas in Australia, Dick Brewer was conceiving a new type of surfboard on Maui. Brewer was the prototype underground surfboard builder, a guru, literally, to a small group of the best young surfers. A second-generation engineer and machinist, his occupation crossed over into his predilection

in the early '60s, as Brewer joined the migratory flock of Californians that didn't come back. He founded Surfboards Hawaii, the first surf shop on Oahu's North Shore, in the winter of '60–'61 and soon became one of the leading makers of the "big guns" used to ride the big winter surf. Later, he wound up shaping for Bing Surfboards in the South Bay, earning notoriety as the craftsman behind David Nuuhiwa's boards.

Since 1966, Brewer had worked at integrating the disciplines of shaping, yoga, and mind-altering drugs into a new vision of surfing that paralleled what had been happening in Byron Bay, Australia. But Brewer was operating in a very different wave environment. His 1967 "mini-gun" surfboard was essentially the opposite of McTavish's Greenough-inspired designs, but also short, light, and radically new. Brewer's boards were teardrop-shaped with the wide point forward, tapering back to narrow pintails. These "pocket rockets" were specialized tools for riding Hawaii's fast, hollow, and powerful waves.

This late-'60s Challenger Surfboards ad (top) reflected the spirit of the times. Griffin created the poster above for Five Summer Stories, *the 1972 MacGillivray-Freeman surf film embodied and articulated the values of the late-1960s.*

Shaping guru, Dick Brewer, 1968.

< Surfing Goes Underground >

The revolution was diverted almost as soon as it began. Surfing's radical fringe found itself increasingly isolated in the post-psychedelic '70s, as vested interests in the sport regrouped, retooled, and restyled to capitalize on an activity that fed the most exciting and charismatic subcultures on the planet. Surf culture began to look like potential big business, and the capitalists began to move in. As Phil Dexter, visionary president of Big Surf, Inc., who built the first man-made wave machine in the desert of Arizona (1969), would say, "Who needs an ocean?"

Perhaps as an indicator for the species, perhaps simply as misanthrope, Mickey Dora loathed surfing contests and the fascist control they exercised over the surfers, beaches, and waves. He characterized contest judges as "senile surf freaks." At the World Contest in Puerto Rico in 1968, the panel of judges ignored the new aesthetic of free and radical expression and delivered a verdict based on classic old-school criteria: Hawaii's Fred Hemmings Jr., a former Makaha champ, rode the biggest waves for the longest distances to win a hairsbreadth decision over Midget Farrelly. In the midst of it all, diminutive Dick Brewer–protege Reno Abellira administered a future-shock speed-surfing performance but wiped out several times. The failure of the new school of surfing to win recognition in Puerto Rico dovetailed with a generational rejection of authority and a growing apathy towards competition.

While Hawaii fielded a team for the 1970 World Contest in Victoria, Australia, the Island surfers knew it wasn't likely they could win in Australia unless the waves were huge. Their interest in international competitions held in small waves was minimal. "This is between the Australians and the Californians" seemed to be the attitude, and the best of them were caught up in a reverie of surfboard development, lifestyle experimentation, and big-wave acid tests. Conservative champ Fred Hemmings wasn't alone in his unwillingness to travel six thousand miles to defend his title in the remote outpost of Bell's Beach. Once was enough.

Of course, not everyone stayed away from the 1970 World Contest. In May 1970, the arrival of a couple hundred hot surfers in the small town of Torquay kicked off a bizarre two weeks of cultural crisis. There were raids and drug busts, politics and walkouts, crises and confusion, bad behavior and, to make matters worse, almost no surf. Forget that Corky Carroll verbally abused the wife of the local innkeeper, that all but one of the U.S. "continental" team refused to march in the opening

Owl Chapman casually slotted on the world's fastest wave, Maalaea on Maui, in 1976. "I've got a lot of alcohol in me here," he later commented.

Opposite: The shortboard revolution ushered in a new era of experimentation. (Top) Famous power surfer Barry Kanaiaupuni loose in the juice at Honolua Bay, January 1972. Left: On the North Shore, sugar heir and stepson to Clark Gable, Bunker Spreckels translated the revolution into personal terms. Dancing at the edge of the impossible, this 20-year-old kid rode tiny, thick, weird little boards deep in the bowels of the heaviest barrels, amazing everyone with his utter lack of fear.

parade, that David Nuuhiwa flew back to California in a huff after being eliminated in an early round (and while he was in flight, officials decided everyone would get a second chance), and that everyone said the whole thing was a joke. Something magical happened anyway.

At the eleventh hour, faced with a flat ocean and no champion, International Surfing Federation (ISF) president Eduardo Arena reluctantly agreed to move the semifinals and finals two hours east to a remote "secret spot" with an excellent exposure to waves coming up out of the Tasman Sea. There, near a farming community called Johanna, the world's best surfers gathered in a bucolic seaside setting to compete. On hand were only the few remaining competitors, the odd friend or companion, a few members of the surf media, a couple of ISF officials, five judges, a half-dozen farm families, and several grazing Jersey cows. In fading afternoon light and clean six-foot surf, Rolf Aurness proved his point (that shortboards had gone too far: Aurness rode a longer board for better paddling and glide) and left everyone else pondering. "Nothing can detract from Rolf's win," wrote John Witzig. "He was far and away the most consistent and aggressive and exciting surfer. There were no detractors of his victory . . . that was the best thing about the contest."

Accepting his trophy at a simple ceremony at the nearby Lorne Hotel, Rolf said simply, "This is out-asight!" And then he left. It was like the day the music died. He walked off with his trophy, and he never competed again; he became a reclusive "soul surfer," and it was like the championship didn't mean a thing. Rejecting the "gaudy metal and ego trips" of competition, Wayne Lynch, Nat Young, Ted Spencer, and other Aussies moved off into the seclusion of the country. In Hawaii and California it was much the same thing.

On the release of his decade-closing *Pacific Vibrations,* John Severson described his goals in the film: "An example of man in harmony with nature. A film to remind you of your roots. A life that doesn't emphasize materialism. Have a good time. The natural way. A witness to the truth."

Surfing at Trestles on the Camp Pendleton Marine reservation in the 1960s and 1970s meant arrest and confiscation . . . if you were caught.

It was almost as if surfing, like the counterculture, was going under-ground. Surf music was dead, and the music of the late '60s was Led Zeppelin, John Mayall, and Jimi Hendrix. Surfers like Mike Hynson, David Nuuhiwa, Leslie Potts, and Chris Green, who reputedly felt a common bond with the brothers in the "Brotherhood," were friends and inspirations to Hendrix, who assembled a word-of-mouth concert and "be-in" on the slopes of Maui's Haleakala crater in 1970 in a last-ditch attempt to cross the "Rainbow Bridge" before the unique window of the psychedelic '60s closed. A week later Hendrix was dead, and the film *Rainbow Bridge* was all that remained.

Meanwhile, the surf industry appeared to be collapsing; clubs and organizations were losing membership or dissolving as the sport dis-persed into enclaves of localism amid rumors of environmental disas-ter and the background roar of Vietnam. There was a medieval taste in the air; the past was dying, the future was incubating.

<White House Breaks>

In California, young Rolf Aurness (son of television's James *Gunsmoke* Arness) was on a tear, dominating the AAAA circuit with a loose unconcerned ease that baffled his more hard-minded foes. At the time, Rolf and his friend Corky Carroll were the only two surfers with professional dispensation to surf at Cotton's Point, where Aurness lived. The old Cotton estate had recently become the Western White House, and when Richard Milhous Nixon (the dude from Yorba Linda) was in town, the beach in front of his palatial abode was off-limits. Whether or not the Hobie surfboard they presented to the president was a factor in the Aurness-Carroll exemption, no one was saying.

On one occasion, when less notable surfers were enjoying perfect eight-foot waves down the beach at Trestles (which was off-limits any-way, but with Nixon in town it was doubly off-limits), an eighty-five-foot

The finals of the 1970 World Contest were held at a remote beach in Victoria, Australia, on the Tasman Sea. Won by Californian Rolf Aurness (son of Gunsmoke's Jim Arness), the event seemed to showcase the intimate and personal nature of surfing rather than its popular face. Above: Aurness winning at Johanna. Left: Rolf at Malibu, summer of 1969, during his AAAA rampage to the title.

Coast Guard craft was used to nudge the waveriders towards shore and into the waiting arms of the MPs. The concerns of surfers, however, were well beneath the sloping nose of the free-world leader and his beach-roaming security staff.

Fortunately for Nixon, the man next door with the large apparatus was not preparing to volley bazooka rounds onto the presidential grounds. It was merely a 1000mm Century telephoto lens, and the neighbor was merely a friendly paparazzo, dealing his photos off to *Life* magazine, in which he himself had been featured a couple of times in the '60s. The neighbor was *Surfer* founder John Severson.

The Surf Spot

Where the happy coincidence of almost infinite variables creates surf of excellent quality in an accessible and relatively safe environment, that place is a surf spot. Scattered around the world are thousands of such spots, and they vary enormously. There are the famous classic point breaks, like California's Malibu, South Africa's Jeffreys Bay, and Australia's Byron Bay. There are the notoriously powerful big-wave breaks—Hawaii's Waimea Bay, California's Mavericks at Half Moon Bay, Baja Mexico's Todos Santos Island, and South Africa's Dungeons. And then there are the elegant but hard-breaking reef breaks, like Grajagan in Java, Uluwatu in Bali, and the prototypical Banzai Pipeline on Oahu's celebrated North Shore—waves so refined and perfectly formed that their peeling progress is like poetry to watch.

The thing is, every surf spot has its day. The right tide, the right swell, the right help from a breeze from just the right direction, and a surf spot can be transformed into brief perfection—for a day or an hour or perhaps just a single wave. A listing of all the world's surf spots would probably be as lengthy as a mid-sized town's residential telephone directory. Of course, a lot of names would be unlisted. Surfers call those "secret spots."

One of the most perfect wave spots in the world is Honolua Bay on the western end of Maui. Here, waves fan into the Molokai Channel from a North Pacific storm to peel smoothly along the reef.

Above: Paddlers watch a dolphin drop into a wave.

From Soul to Pro

< From Soul to Pro >

"It would seem that the sport of surfing is growing towards a greater level of recognition by people not so much connected with the surfing world per se, but that of the business world, where advertising is one of the key factors for success. Frankly, I wouldn't mind taking home 7,000 bucks for finishing eighth place in a commercially organized, sponsored surfing tournament. It's a hell of a lot better than digging ditches or driving a honey wagon."

—Bill Hamilton, *Surfer* magazine, 1971.

The apparently innocuous introduction of the surfboard leash (a.k.a. "kook cord") in 1971 had a huge impact on surfing. At first rejected out of hand by the "soul surfers," purists who wanted surfing to remain as pristine and uncluttered as possible, the prospect of not losing your surfboard in a wipeout (and having to swim in after it) ultimately had an irresistible appeal. After its first appearance in Santa Cruz, the idea spread—slowly at first. It simply wasn't cool to have this *leash* hanging off of your board, not to mention that your board could snap back and knock your teeth out. Real men didn't use leashes.

But the board didn't snap back too often, and when a leashed surfer wiped out, his board didn't tumble through crowds of paddling surfers like a loose saber. The leash actually made things safer and, though it was banned mid-contest at the Malibu AAAA in summer of '71, it was eventually accepted by surfers everywhere.

Once a comfort zone was reached with the leash, the developmental curve of performance soared. It opened the doors to experimentation. You could try a wildly spectacular move knowing that, if you blew it, you wouldn't have to swim. This, coupled with dramatic improvements in wetsuits (lighter, warmer, more flexible), allowed surfers unprecedented opportunities to improve their technique. Suddenly everyone was "going for it." The tube ride (a low-percentage maneuver and largely unachievable Holy Grail) became the performance focus of the 1970s and beyond, mainly because of the leash. Paddling and swimming abilities—basic traditional "waterman" skills—began to play less of a role; technology was domesticating the sport of Hawaiian kings.

Country Surfboards in Haleiwa, 1971, with Rick "Black" Kalinowski the embodiment of soul and cool. Top: And yes, surfing again.

< The Boogie Board >

At first conceived as a sort of entry-level surf toy—a sort of Volksurfboard—the Boogie Board was soon taken into the extreme surf conditions favored by body-surfers, where the little boards' softness and flexibility made riding hollow waves in shallow water much safer. One of the greatest Boogie Boarders is Mike Stewart, shown here at Backdoor Pipeline.

Another milestone in the annals of saltwater democracy was the Boogie Board™, created by an engineer-turned-watertoy conceptualizer named Tom Morey, who bailed from Ventura and wound up on the Big Island. Morey was a man with a multitude of ideas. He designed boards with air intakes, multiple flutes, bizarre Neptunian outline shapes, and all manner of odd fins and keels. He fantasized air-lubricated, motorized boards that skimmed along on time-release sodium bicarbonate bubbles. His ruminations and illustrations appeared in *Surfer*—fun stuff, but none of it was *really* gonna happen. But then something did.

He was living in Kona, his wife was pregnant, and it was hot. "I had no money, and the surf was good right off of the front yard, and I had some of this polyethylene foam in the garage—it was left over from doing the things for the article—so I got out the *Honolulu Advertiser* and an electric carving knife and an iron, and I cut out a little four-and-a-half-foot-long board with the knife, and then I ironed the foam [to seal it] with the newspaper in between, and the print of the newspaper transferred to the board, and that's how I know the date." It was July 7, 1971.

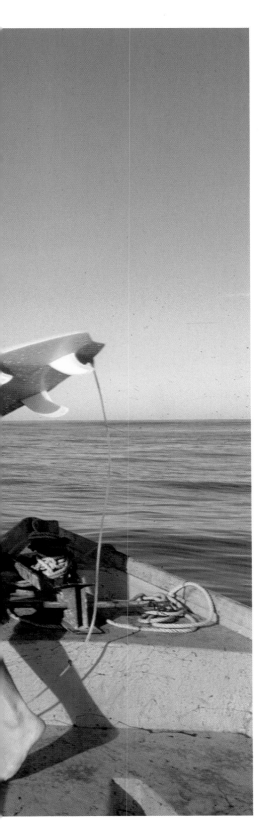

Morey paddled out; by now the surf was "crappy, but I could *feel* the wave; I could *feel* the motion of the surf, and here was this board with no fin just snakin' along." He nicknamed his new creation the S.N.A.K.E. for Side, Navel, Arm, Knee, and Elbow, since he rode it prone, and all those body parts and more were picking up sensations of the wave. He ended up calling his new thing (in a somewhat smaller version) a "Boogie Board." It made an impact right away, especially with kids. Soft, light, compact, and ding-proof, it created a new kind of relationship with the ocean and turned millions of people into riders of waves.

The Boogie Board proved to be a sort of "Volksurfboard." It's gotten virtually every kid in striking range of a beach out into the waves. But Morey thinks that even now, over thirty years later, it's just beginning. "If you think there's a lot of people in the water now, you haven't seen anything yet. Someday everybody in the world will have a Boogie Board in the house. They're cheap, they're portable; you can take 'em to the pool, the river, the lake, the beach . . . and it's not gonna stop on this planet."

< The Worldwide Search for Perfection >

Surfers are nomads. To surf is to seek, and to seek is to roam. To find a good wave might require traveling a good distance. To find a great, uncrowded wave might take you to the ends of the earth. Bruce Brown's *The Endless Summer* actually recapitulated and promulgated the core ritual of surf culture: the search for the perfect wave.

The perfect wave is not just a perfect wave; it's the perfect place, the perfect time, and the perfect conditions. Some surfers never find it, many just once or twice in their lives. Others find it (surprise!) at their local surf spots. But for those who really go after it, the stories are legend.

The nascent travel adventures of the '50s, from the marathon coastal explorations of Bob Simmons to the first Makaha and North Shore beachheads, established a solid nomadic ideology. Bud Browne went wave-hunting to Australia in the '50s. He was followed by Bruce Brown and the boys, who paddled the first surfboards into the waves of West Africa. They were followed a couple of years later by Englishman Rodney Sumpter, who toured the Ivory Coast and other West African environs. Then came the redoubtable team of Kevin Naughton and Craig Peterson with their invincible Brazilian compatriot, Tito Rosemberg. Greg MacGillivray and Jim Freeman helped Mark Martinson and Bill Hamilton fill their passports with stamps in the '60s, making *Free and Easy* and *Waves of Change,* and soon dozens of moviemakers and magazine photographers were touring the world with surf stars in tow, searching for the new discovery—the perfect wave—that would sell tickets or magazines.

As the domesticated beaches of the world became more crowded, the surf safari (the quest to find the undiscovered or uncrowded surf) became an essential part of the surfing experience. The surfing magazines devoted increasing space to travel adventures, with annual travel issues crammed with global forays. From the humorous Rick Griffin and Ron Stoner travel adventures of the '60s to photojournalist Bernie Baker's groundbreaking (and surfbreaking) journey through Central America in 1970 ("Perils of the Tropics" in *Surfer*), to the delightfully scruffy travels of Kevin Naughton and Craig Peterson in Central America, West Africa, Morocco, Spain, France, Ireland, Mexico, and Fiji, the contemporary jet-set world of surfing was pioneered by adventurous individuals with an itch for waves and wandering. But sometimes travel brought other, more illicit rewards.

The essence of the search: Kevin Naughton finds what he's looking for at Cloudbreak off Tavarua Island, Fiji, 1984.

< Surf Culture and Drug Culture >

Marijuana had long been a common ingredient of the smoke from driftwood fires. Drugs and alcohol went hand in hand with the free-association mentality of the beach, and surfing's position of the cultural borderlands had long connected it to the beats, bikers, and other fringe dwellers. Surfing was always about freedom and experimentation, and the no-man's-land of the beach was a good place to bring your bottle, your joint, or your needle. Out here on the sand, laws were laughed at, instructive signage was target material for paint or bullet, and the cops never came around because they just *knew* they were out of place.

Steve Pezman interviewed psychedelic guru Timothy Leary for Surfer in 1978. Leary described surfing as "the spiritual aesthetic style of the liberated self," adding: "I've picked out as my symbol . . . a surfer right at that point moving along constantly right at the edge of the tube. That position is the metaphor of life to me, the highly conscious life."

There had always been cheap marijuana south of the border, but with the psychedelic revolution of the '60s and the soul-surfing era of the early '70s, demand for drugs had become huge in the United States (and elsewhere), and the surfers' nomadic lifestyle and free-spirited outlook put them in the right place at the right time to participate in some entrepreneurial ebb and flow.

In the mid-'60s, several surfers with experience in small, mostly Mexican-border smuggles had coalesced into the Brotherhood of Light and established an international drug-trafficking operation dealing marijuana, hashish, pure LSD, and other psychedelics to the

surfing world. By the end of the decade, the Brotherhood was a large network of investors, organizers, traffickers, and dealers, but the people who were still out there taking the big risks—getting their hands on the drugs in dangerous parts of the world—were often the traveling surfers.

One prominent big-wave rider of the '60s—a polished, polite young man—learned that smuggling for the Brotherhood was a good way to make a lot of money fast. On his first assignment, he and his girlfriend posed as rich American newlyweds, flying first-class to Germany, where they purchased a new Mercedes and made their way by road and ship (five-star accommodations all the way) to Afghanistan, where they checked into Kabul's finest hotel. There, while they dined in the finest style, the car was taken from the garage, the rocker panels were cut and removed, the body was packed with hashish and hash oil, and the car was welded back together, sanded,

Surf explorers Kevin Naughton and Tito Rosemberg (above) met in Morocco in January '75. Travel brings surfers together at remote spots around the world, drawn by the allure of perfect, uncrowded surf. Travel also introduces surfing to the uninitiated.

perfectly repainted, and returned before morning. The couple then left the hotel and continued their five-star honeymoon journey as far as Karachi, where they put the Mercedes on a boat bound for Long Beach, California, then took a taxi to the airport and flew home, first-class.

Left: In the early 1970s, the Coast Highway out in front of Laguna Beach's Sound Spectrum was frequently jammed with hordes of hippies, attracted to town by the rainbow message of the Brotherhood of Eternal Light.

That was the easy part. Now he had to wait till the car arrived, cleared customs, and was ready to pick up. Only then, when he came for the car, would he know if they'd been successful. As it happened, it was the beginning of a long, cautious, and successful smuggling career. He was finally caught in a small-time marijuana bust in California, turned state's evidence to minimize his own sentence, and continues to live in fear of retribution from those he helped put away.

Right: A West African reads Surfer *in 1972.*

In *Mr. Sunset* (1997), Phil Jarratt recounts the life story of pro surfer Jeff Hakman, including tales of harrowing drug-smuggling runs, beginning when he was a team rider for Plastic Fantastic, the hottest California surfboard brand of the psychedelic era. When Hakman discovered other team riders were importing hashish across the border from Mexico in "channeled" (hollowed-out) surfboards, he was persuaded to make a run, too. At the border, hot sun combined with a crack in the fiberglass caused the black hash oil to ooze out of one of the boards, but officials didn't notice and he made it through okay. Despite the close call, Hakman went on to a couple of very heavy deals (including runs in Lebanon and Thailand), a bust, some jail time—and eventually heroin addiction.

The Hakman Connection

Jeff Hakman was the best competitive surfer for a decade, from his win at the 1965 Kahanamoku Invitational to his victory at the '76 Bells Beach contest in Australia, where he won in the throes of a heroin binge. It was after the latter event, in the town of Torquay, that he reached an agreement with Alan Green to license him and his business-minded friend Bob McKnight (with financial backing from McKnight's father) to distribute the unique Quiksilver "boardshorts" in America.

The trunks' unique design (yoke-style scalloped legs and a wide waistband) was perfect for surfing and dovetailed with a strong surge of Australian influence in the sport to become the hottest thing in surf fashion, circa '76–'78. Hakman and McKnight made a pile of money, but Jeff's battle with a lifelong monkey eventually drove him out of the company and nearly out of surfing. He reestablished relations with both some ten years later when he partnered up with Harry Hodge (the high-rolling, free-wheelin' filmmaker who made the film *Band on the Run* in the '70s) on the wildly successful "boarding company" Quiksilver Europe (a.k.a. Quiksilver Na Pali), with sales of $72 million in 1996.

As professional as they come, Jeff Hakman continued to turn in phenomenal performances while struggling with his addiction. Smirnoff Pro-Am at Waimea Bay, Thanksgiving Day, 1974.

Things got pretty hot in Hawaii back in the mid-'70s, and Hakman and associates weren't the only surfers in the thick of it. Boards packed with cocaine were coming in from Peru (the white crystalline powder was almost identical in appearance to the urethane foam), then shipped on to California. Thai pot was coming in with servicemen from Vietnam or "vacationing" surfers. Maui Wowie and Big Island "bud" were everywhere. Hash, opium, and heroin had been coming through Hawaii from Southeast Asia for many years, except now surfers were involved, and it was having a noticeable effect on some major players. The greatest Australian surfer of the period, Michael Peterson, was feeding a heavy drug habit and soon retreated into institutional oblivion, as did *Surfer* magazine's great photographer, Ron Stoner.

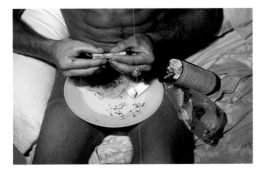

"Genetic space child" Bunker Spreckels was dead by 1977 of an experimental life that never operated below the red-line.

Mobility and lack of structure in the surfing lifestyle made for a convenient crossover from surf culture to drug culture, and a number of surfers have been casualties or survivors over the years. Top: Deep into Mexico, California surfers found great waves and good pot (a false bottom in the WD-40 can hides the stash, c. 1976). Meanwhile, East Coast star and Bali pioneer Rick Rasmussen (above) was gunned down in a Harlem incident.

It got uglier. East Coast champion Rick Rasmussen, an early Bali surfer, was shot dead on a Harlem street corner while trying to score some smack. Small-time surfer-smugglers were cutting into lines of distribution they didn't even know existed. One night a haole surfer was beaten on the North Shore then tied into a chair and held at gunpoint while his girlfriend was raped by each of the assailants multiple times. Surfing was not looking entirely like a clean, healthy sport, and Hawaii was starting to seem more like paradox than paradise.

As the action got meaner and the crowds got thicker, a new element entered the scene in the early '70s: Christian surfers. Surf with Jesus. Team Jesus. A lot of surfers all over the world took the drop into God's chosen wave in reaction to the directionless backwash of the '60s. Other surfers started looking for new waves, and they found them. Everywhere. Deeper Baja and mainland Mexico, the Caribbean, Morocco, South Africa, France, Japan, the South Pacific, and the magic discovery of Uluwatu, the beautiful barreling left on Bali, an exotic Buddhist island off the eastern tip of Java. It turned out the world had a lot more surf than anyone had expected.

< Uluwatu >

The world was first alerted to Bali's surf potential in 1970 when a Qantas steward wrote to Bob Evans at *Australian Surfing Life* magazine to report excellent waves in the Denpasar Airport area. The film-maker flew up with Mark Warren and Col Smith, and the two Sydney surfers were soon shown ripping the waves at Kuta Beach in Evans' 1971 movie, *Family Free*. Tipped off to the potential, fellow Aussie filmmakers Alby Falzon and David Elfick arrived with young Stephen Cooney and the American big-wave surfer Rusty Miller in tow.

It was Falzon who discovered the tortuous trail down the sheer cliff (later named Hamburger Hill) and the secret passage through the surf-flushed cave to the mystic waves of Uluwatu. All was revealed in the free-spirited surf film *Morning of the Earth*. (Falzon, Elfick, and Phil Jarratt went on to found *Tracks*, the most influential Australian surf publication.)

The Balinese people had an enormous respect for and fear of the ocean, and they were dumbfounded and amazed to see these argonauts go forth into the unforgiving brine with their exotic lightweight spear-boats. Island men and boys competed intensely for the right to carry the surfers' boards down

Waiting for surf in Bali while filming Morning of the Earth, *Alby Falzon and his two surf stars, 15-year-old Stephen Cooney and recent American expatriate Rusty Miller, visited a remote temple and in the process discovered the mystic left-hander, Uluwatu. Peter McCabe (above) was one of the early beneficiaries of their discovery.*

the long trail to the waves. The surfers were treated like gods—accompanied through the villages by gamelan music and crowds of colorful natives. After coming here with Hakman to surf for Dick Hoole and Jack McCoy's *In Search of Tubular Swells,* Gerry Lopez rhapsodized about the waves and people and the guerrilla-surf lifestyle of Bali in the surfing press. But Bali, like plenty of other stops on the global surf tour, was replete with drugs—high-grade marijuana, hash, magic mushrooms, cocaine, heroin—the full spectrum.

Bali opened the door to a new quality and scale of surf travel. As discoveries followed in Java and other parts of Indonesia, and later the Indian Ocean and the Philippines, it wasn't just trips to Hawaii for the winter any more. It was exploration and discovery by boat or Jeep or float plane or whatever. By the 1980s, it seemed like everyone was traveling. In the immortal words of Owl Chapman, "A local is just a dirtbag who can't get his shit together to travel."

< Discovery in Java >

In July of 1972, Californian Bob Laverty looked down from a weather-diverted Djakarta-to-Bali flight and spotted a magic curving reefline 30,000 feet below in a remote national sanctuary called the Plengkung Forest Reserve. With fellow surfer Bill Boyum, he planned and executed the first recorded surf expedition into the place, utilizing Suzuki 80s as pack mules, traveling by ferry to Java and by bikes to Grajagan village. They loaded the bikes onto two primitive fishing boats to get across the lagoon to the reserve, then rode the bikes along the beach until they got bogged down in sand and coral. They proceeded on foot, through dense shoreline jungle with its big cats and monkeys, and finally collapsed, exhausted, in the black of night. They awoke to the sight of perfect six- to eight-foot barrels peeling down the reef for hundreds of yards right in front of them.

Bill's savvy brother Mike cut through mountains of international red tape to create a surf camp at the spot, now called G-Land, where a couple dozen surfers at a time live in comfortable tree houses, enjoy athletes' meals, and surf their brains out on these amazing tropical waves.

Spotted by Bob Laverty on a flight from Djakarta to Bali, the perfect waves of Grajagan proved one of the great surf discoveries of all time. Since repeatedly upgraded, it proved the model of many such camps to follow.

123

<Gerry Lopez>

Always privy to the foibles of his surfing friends, Gerry Lopez never seemed to lose his focus or succumb to the temptations of the drug world. He kept himself in shape, practiced self-discipline, and maintained his "center" while others struggled with temptation and lost. Born and raised in Honolulu, of Cuban-German-Japanese descent, Lopez grew up riding the waves at Waikiki, graduated to the North Shore, and began to make an impression at age twenty in the winter of '68–'69. A calculating contest surfer, he did well and made the Hawaiian World Contest teams in '70 and '72. But the real contest for him was the Pipeline, where he became the undisputed master of the barrel, establishing the tube ride as surfing's ultimate maneuver and the Pipeline as surfing's most perfect tube. An early disciple of Dick Brewer's psychedelic Zen approach to surfing, Lopez soon found his own path.

He was shaping for a company called Surfline in Honolulu when he and salesman Jack Shipley decided to start a new surfboard company,

Lightning Bolt. Driven by Lopez's powerful charisma and talent, a loose confederation of independent surfer/shapers gathered under the Bolt emblem. Guided by Hang Ten founder Duke Boyd, Bolt's logo became the most powerful symbol in surfing in the mid-'70s. "Duke made Gerry a god," says Rory Russell, the Pipeline runner-up in those years.

Featured in three of the best surf films of the decade—*Five Summer Stories* (1972), *Hot Lips and Inner Tubes* (1976), and *Free Ride* (1978)—Lopez got to play himself in writer/director John Milius' 1978 treatment of Malibu as Greek tragedy, *Big Wednesday*. Milius, an old Malibu surfer himself, liked Gerry's work and cast him as Arnold Schwartzenegger's sidekick, Subotai, in his 1980 comic-inspired adventure, *Conan the Barbarian*. Lopez went on to play a near-mute Dayak warrior opposite Nick Nolte in Milius's *Farewell to the King* (1989).

"The Dayaks are natives of Borneo," Milius explained in a 1992 interview. "They're masters of the jungle, yet Gerry was more graceful than them . . . more silent. He'd climb right up a nut tree and sit on a branch—he always appears to be moving slowly, but he's really quite fast. And he learns so fast! Like in *Conan*, Gerry would be first to learn the swordsmanship, then he taught Arnold and the others. He's amazing, really. He can run 40 miles, swim wherever he has to."

Says Lopez in partial explanation: "Surfing forces you to focus on the here and now. . . . Here and now and what's coming now. That's one of the biggest lessons for anyone. So many live in recollection and anticipation, but you've gotta be focused on where your foot's going right now."

There have been a succession of surfers who have so mastered the challenging tubes of Banzai Beach they've earned the title of "Mr. Pipeline." First there was Phil Edwards, then Butch Van Artsdalen, then Jock Sutherland, and then Gerry Lopez, whose supreme wave judgment and eloquent precision reflected his total mastery of the place (sequence). Seeking out similar waves in other parts of the world led Lopez to Bali, Java, and Fiji. Opposite: Cloudbreak in Fiji. Above: Lopez as Dayak in Farewell to the King.

< Money for Nothin', Chicks for Free >

The soul of surfing may be wandering, but its heart has always been Hawaii. There's just no better, more intense surf (not to mention the perfect climate and golden beaches of the highest order) anywhere on

the planet. Even in the midst of its dispersion, surfing strengthened its connection to the sport's true Mecca, the stretch of Oahu coastline between Laniakea and Sunset Beach on the North Shore, often called the seven-mile miracle. Hawaii remained the ultimate proving ground, and each winter surfers arrived from all over the world, and each spring many of them hadn't gone home. Instead, they stayed and became firemen, lifeguards, carpenters, roofers, teachers, fishermen . . . they did anything to remain.

In the early '70s, there were a couple of small shops on the North Shore—Country Surfboards in Haleiwa, later a small shop at Sunset Beach near Kammie's Market. Most boards were made in town (Honolulu), but a lot were made in garages and sheds, too. With so much experimenting going on, surfers started to accumulate a collection of boards—a quiver designed to fit a variety of conditions, each board built for a specific range and use—smaller, wider, curvier boards for smaller surf; longer, narrower, straighter boards for bigger surf—and to provide backups when powerful waves snapped fragile sticks.

Above: Surfing reentered the mainstream in the 1970s, thanks to ex-Malibu gremmie and director John Milius, with Big Wednesday *(1978) and* Apocalypse Now *(1979). The title* Big Wednesday *was already familiar with surfers who'd seen John Severson's so-titled 1961 surf movie.*

Style and attitude shifted as aromas of professionalism wafted onto the surf scene in the 1970s. Surfers did whatever it took to be noticed and come out on top. Far left: Larry Bertlemann (with afro and Rolls) was a pioneer with attitude. A Duke Kahanamoku Invitational champion, he was heavily influential in the skateboard revolution of the early 1970s, especially with the Zephyr team and their South Bay "Dogtown" scene.

Above left: Tools of the trade at the Smirnoff Pro-Am, one of the first events to offer significant prize money in the early 1970s. These three boards (extensions of traditional guns and Dick Brewer's mini-gun concept) lie poised to conquer the giant waves of Waimea Bay.

Left: Wayne "Rabbit" Bartholomew spearheaded the mid-1970s Australian "backside attack" on the North Shore with an attitude the presaged the pro surfing tour (of which, by the year 2002, he was president).

Every swell that hit the North Shore was both an expression session and a test drive. During contest season (roughly November through January), the day-to-day pressure was greatly increased by having a thousand of the best surfers in the world confined to a relatively small sandbox. Out in the water, waves were at a premium, the winter sessions dominated by Hawaiians—Hakman, Barry Kanaiaupuni, Jock Sutherland (back from an incomprehensible stint in the Army at the pinnacle of his powers), Lopez, Sam Hawk, Eddie Aikau, Owl Chapman, Tom Stone, James Jones, and a rapidly maturing Reno Abellira. There were only a few stellar visitors, like Australian Terry Fitzgerald (the Sultan of Speed), South African Gavin Rudolph, and Californian Mike Doyle.

But by 1975, things had shifted as a group of Southern Hemi surfers came in with determination and plenty of attitude to stage a self-described "backside attack" at the Pipeline. They took on the biggest, meanest waves with an aggression usually reserved for goofy-foot (right foot forward) surfers at the spot. The hot performers were the Tomson cousins, Shaun and Mike, from South Africa and a pack of Aussies—Peter Townend, Ian Cairns, Mark Warren, Bruce Raymond, and the very unique Queenslander Wayne "Rabbit" Bartholomew, whose cultural guru at the time was David "Ch-ch-ch-ch-changes" Bowie. These guys were great surfers, not only at Pipeline but also at Sunset and Waimea. In interviews and articles they asserted that the way you prove yourself in surfing is to go to the North Shore, take off on the biggest, gnarliest waves, make 'em, and talk about it afterward. Fame!

"Their dream," wrote *Surfer* magazine, "was of a world where all you did was surf; then the thing you loved became the thing you did. They called it professional surfing, and despite a grumpy soul-daddy backlash, their act changed the way surfers everywhere regarded themselves."

Such self-assertion on Hawaiian turf reaped a predictable reward. Rabbit got his front teeth knocked out and the most prominent Aussies, after receiving death threats, spent the winter of '76-'77 holed up with the indigenous spirits at the Kuilima Hotel, which had been built over an ancient *heiau*.

Even so, this down under crew ruled the press with their risky surfing and stimulating soundbites, and their effect on surfing was electrifying. They brought the color back into a soulfully understated sport, and with the color came the money and the attention and even more concentration on the North Shore. In the winter of '77–'78, director John Milius showed up to film the Hawaiian segments of *Big*

Wednesday. While the surf fad of the '60s had long died out (though it thrived worldwide in the heating-up skateboard scene) and the movie was no box-office bonanza, the vortex of energy Milius created on the North Shore had a galvanizing effect, and the movie's emphasis on the BIG wave created a subtle shift in the sport's development. After years of media domination by the expressive, stylish surfers who excelled in small and medium waves, the big-wave riders began to get new respect, and even more surfers were drawn to the North Shore's winter surf.

Big Wednesday also meant big business, at least bigger than the scale surfers were used to. With only an annual total of $150,000 prize money in pro surf contests and few lucrative sponsorship deals available, the production of the film (in Costa Rica as well as Hawaii) brought a new kind of employment (albeit temporary) for surfers, photographers, lifeguards, shapers, and peripheral personnel. Bud Browne, Greg Mac-Gillivray, Gerry Lopez, Billy Hamilton, George Greenough, Ian Cairns, Peter Townend, Denny Aaberg (Malibu golden-era surfer and co-author of the script with Milius), and a slew of others got into the project, and the enterprise became a valuable learning experience that opened the doors to later Hollywood involvement in surfing and the North Shore.

Right: One of the most brilliant big-wave surfers of all time, Eddie Aikau appears deeply committed to the peak at Waimea Bay, December 1973. No one else surfed huge waves with such casual style.

Above: The Aikau family is one of the core local surf tribes on Oahu. Eddie, crouched on the left next to brother Clyde, drowned paddling for help when the modern voyaging canoe Hokule'a *got into trouble in a storm in the Moloka'i Channel. The rest of the crew was rescued and the canoe salvaged. A memorial big-wave contest (The Quiksilver In Memory of Eddie Aikau) is scheduled each winter in Hawaii—but the event is only run if the waves reach 20 feet or above. The contest is referred to by surfers simply as "The Eddie."*

< Surf Sells, the Culture Quickens >

By the late '70s, catalyzed by brash Australian energy, the film *Big Wednesday* and a few widely distributed surf films such as *Five Summer Stories* and *Free Ride*, the sport of surfing started creeping back into mainstream consciousness. Back in Newport Beach, California, where a number of surfwear companies and many successful surf shops were located, surfers started to counter the Australian influence with bold, radical small-wave surfing and bright, colorful wetsuits and clothes. Among the kids haunting Newport's "hottest hundred yards" of jetties and tubes was trendmaker Danny Kwock; a surfer with bold sense of style, he would become VP of advertising and marketing for Quiksilver USA. Meanwhile, several other top surfers got into the rag business, notably Michael Tomson, who started Gotcha Sportswear; his cousin Shaun, who started Instinct (and later Solitude); and Southern California shaper and artist Shawn Stüssy.

In fact, these and other surf-based companies were benefiting mightily from the surging popularity of skateboarding (thanks to the advent of urethane wheels and the highly visual hotdog maneuvers they made possible for pool, pipe, and ramp skaters) was adding to the numbers, and the legions of new young Boogie Boarders wanted surfwear, too. Surf business was suddenly booming. The surf-related industry trade publication *Action Sports Retailer* commenced publication in January 1980, and

On the surf-film circuit, Bill Delany's Free Ride *(1978) set a new standard for independent sports films while showcasing the sport's emerging professionals.*

130

Left: The successful marketing of surfing in the 1980s put surf company logos on the shirts of people—young and old—all around the world, and surfing contests were drawing more audiences than ever before. Oceanside contest from the pier.

Above: Danny Kwock and a couple of Newport Beach buddies.

co-publishers Jeff Wetmore and Steve Lewis soon launched an annual ASR Trade Show, later Expo. Their tenth anniversary issue was 462 pages.

When windsurfing caught fire in the late '70s, it was more good news for surf business. Invented by a Malibu surfer Hoyle Schweitzer and his sailing buddy Jim Drake back in 1967, the Windsurfer® didn't find an immediate market in the United States, where the sailing surfboard was seen as neither fish nor fowl. But in Europe, where everyone had heard of surfing but few could surf, windsurfing went huge, spawning dozens of copycat manufacturers and an entirely new watersport industry, which finally burst into popularity in the United States in the early '80s with the advent of short, maneuverable boards designed to be sailed in the surf.

While windsurfing would rise and fall rather spectacularly in popularity, snowboarding arrived on the scene at about the same time but suffered no similar fate. Invented and innovated at stages by skiers and surfers alike (notably Mike Doyle, who constructed the first Single Ski in his Leucadia, California, backyard in 1970), this new "board sport" soon flowered into a lucrative winter-season complement to surfing and surf culture.

The infusion of capital into surfing due to the growing success of surf-based apparel companies had a profound effect on every-

The boutiquing of surfing shifted into seriously high gear in the 1980s as wetsuits exploded into color statements and stickers covered everything in sight. The lowly surf shops, too, were revamped and upscaled, reflecting the new status of a sport that was starting to boast a pro circuit with a juicy pot of gold at the end of the rainbow. Costar of The Endless Summer, longtime shaper Robert August parlayed his fame into a successful business. Above, in the late 1970s, his shop reflects the explosive colors of the times. Left: Sticker shock at the Newport Wedge, 1987.

132

Left: Emerging skate culture broadened both the lifestyle and the retail market.
Above: Surf shop in Haleiwa, 1980s.

thing in the sport. As those businesses grew, so did their budgets—for team riders, advertising, movies, videos, television productions, and event sponsorships. Surf culture was in another major transition, and the right thing at the right time could—like foam and *Gidget* or shortboards and drugs— trigger some kind of reaction. Strangely, the next thing to transform the sport subculture was the three-finned surfboard.

133

< The 3-Fin Thruster >

Modern surfing is a function of the modern surfboard. The very short, light, positive (in terms of traction), and thin tri-fin thruster-style surfboard of the 1990s was first developed by Australian Simon Anderson in 1980.

"Gentle Giant" Anderson developed the "3-Fin Thruster" in an attempt to gain some sort of parity in a competition universe dominated by smaller men surfing single- and twin-finned boards on small waves. Anderson and other large competitors simply overpowered these waves and their old boards. But with the thruster design, surfing shifted into a entirely new performance mode, one previously the domain of skateboarders.

The lateral resistance the three fins delivered was so positive that the boards could be ridden with one foot on the tail, directly over the fins. By keeping the body in a steady rhythm of twisting and torquing, a surfer could maneuver higher and deeper on a wave than ever before. That was Anderson's theory, and it proved itself immediately as he dominated in fifteen-foot waves at the 1981 Bells Beach Classic, then took the Coke Contest in Sydney's small waves a few days later. The surfing world switched to thrusters even faster than it did to shortboards in '67–'68.

The surf zone looked a lot different in 1985 than it did in '65. Gone were the longboards and knee-paddlers; no one rolled under the waves like they did in the old days; no more he-man, board-denting death grips while trying to hang on at twelve-foot Sunset. Now the kids just gave a stiff leg thrust as the wave approached, pushed the sharply

Developed at the height of the twin-fin era in 1980, Simon Anderson's three-fin "thruster" surfboard liberated surfers from the "spin-out" problems that dogged the sport from its earliest times. Dubbed "the gentle giant," Anderson proved the design by defeating Cheyne Horan in the finals of the 1981 Rip Curl 3GL Easter Classic in huge Bells Beach surf. Far left: Underwater view of the "thruster" configuration.

135

After watching windsurfers and skateboarders getting "massive air," a few brave surfers began to follow in the footsteps of Larry Bertlemann, developing aerial maneuvers. Aided and abetted by the thruster surfboard, point man in the new air force was Christian Fletcher (right), shown in the summer of '89 at Trestles, which was now a California State Park. The lightweight three-finned boards also allowed female surfers to massively raise the level of their game. Above: State of the art 2001— the Connecticut-born Hawaiian, Megan Abubo.

pointed nose down beneath the surface with a well-timed lunge, and then literally swam the low-volume boards under the wave, popping safely out the back. It was called the "duck dive." If the wave was too big for a duck dive, the surfer just dove under and let the leash snap the board back.

The short, light boards were so extremely maneuverable they were like skateboards. And, like skateboarders, surfers were soon spending less and less time in the water and more and more time in the air. And since the thrusters performed like skateboards, the psychology of skateboarding moved inevitably and irresistibly into the ocean. Tentatively at first, and then with grand abandon, surfing moved out of the tube and into the air. Where Hawaiian Larry Bertlemann had paved the way, Johnny Boy Gomes pushed the envelope even further. In California, Kevin Reed and Davey Smith pulled off some stunning moves, but it was third-generation surfer Christian Fletcher who went off the chart with aerial stunts and functional reinventions of surfing, created by following lines suggested by the waves, but not actually a part of the wave. His maneuvers were, to put a phrase in a word, sick. On five-foot-six-inch boards that weighed less than seven pounds, he was throwing inverted aerial moves and weird flights of fancy straight out of a skateboard park.

< Dueling for Dollars >

Except for the hundred or so years of venereal holocaust and missionary suppression, there has apparently always been competition in surfing. Although paddling anchored the competitive format in the 1930s, and most competition was displaced in the '40s by World War II and its aftermath, when the sport regrouped at Makaha in the early '50s, wave-riding performance had moved onto center stage. The goal was to reward and honor the well-rounded waterman or woman, with surfing as the most prestigious of the disciplines. Cumulative scores for surfing, paddling, tandem surfing, and so on determined the championship.

More recently, surf contests have essentially become surfing contests. Competitors are generally divided into divisions by age, sex, and activity—*menehunes* (small children), boys, juniors, men, masters, seniors, girls, women, tandem, paddle race, professionals—and any other divisions that make sense. As in other sports, there are also divisions by level. Surfing in 2003 has a complex structure of local, regional, state, national, and international competitions. This system was fairly well developed in the '60s, weakened or disintegrated in some areas in the '70s, and reformed and intensified in the '80s and '90s, with forums for the contemporary surfboard and its reemerging polar opposite, the modern longboard.

In the late 1960s, nature-oriented soul surfers were advocating a slow-growth philosophy for the sport and a no-growth philosophy for their own favorite surf spots. They resented the intrusion of

As surfing gained momentum through the '70s and '80s, "professional surfer" began to seem like a potential job description. One of the most successful competitors of all time was Australian Mark Richards (left), a four-time World Champion. On the other hand, local surfers were displaced when the circus pitched its tent on their home turf. The early '70s saw friction between soul surfers and pro surfers, but prize money steadily increased and contests (and pros) prospered.

Surf contests are major events in Santa Cruz, thanks to blufftop spectator seating (left). Since this precarious scene in the 1970s, the cliffs have been fenced, paved, and substantially civilized. Above: ABC's Wide World of Sports *gave pro surfing a big boost with its coverage of Hawaiian contests in the 1960s and '70s. Here James "Booby" Jones is interviewed by Bill Fleming.*

contests and outsiders into their areas. In a 1969 interview with *Surfer* magazine, Mickey Dora, already living much of the year abroad, reportedly scamming a living and on the verge of imminent full expatriatism, said: "The advent of 'professionalism' to the sport will be the final blow. Professionalism will be completely destructive of any control an individual has over the sport at present. These few Wall Street flesh merchants desire to unify surfing only to extract the wealth." "Professionalism is black," chorused Santa Cruz local John Scott in *Surfer*. "Contests only display the hostile commercial polarity."

Surfing definitely changed as the money started coming into competition, a little at first ($28 for "best ride" at the '62 Bells Beach Classic), then more and more—$2,000 for Terry Jones' first-place nose-time at Morey's second noseriding contest in '66; $300 for Corky's win at the first Smirnoff Pro-Am in Santa Cruz in '68, $2,000 for Nat's first place at the Makaha Smirnoff in '70 and $3,000 for Michael Peterson's win at the '74 Coke Surfabout in Sydney; $1,000 total purse for the first Pipeline Masters in '71, $130,000 in 1996 with $20,000 going to the winner, Kelly Slater. There were livelihoods at stake in the business of riding waves; it wasn't just all fun and games anymore.

< The Rise of the World Pro Tour >

Despite all the grumbling and anti-contest sentiment, surfers had to make a living, and some of them would rather make it surfing than doing anything else. It was clear that competition wasn't going away; the question was, what form would it take? The progressive vision of the time was something like tennis or golf. "If surfing could only be like golf," people were saying—with a well-managed, high-paying tour of the world's best surf spots.

During December of 1968, big-wave surfer Fred Van Dyke and television sports producer Larry Lindberg (producer of the television show *Dukes of Hazzard* for ABC) made a modest proposal to a group of top surfers gathered in Waikiki: to become charter members of the International Professional Surfers Association, the goal of which, in Van Dyke's words, would be "to establish a bona-fide world champion through a series of contests around the globe. We would also offer prize money, promote the sport, and protect our members' interests." The model would be the Professional Golf Association (PGA). A rash of great surfers signed letters of intent, Fred Van Dyke was elected president, and Ron Sorrell, an Outrigger Canoe Club member and public relations executive, was named commissioner. Sorrell was convinced there was a future for professional surfing, and that future was spelled TV. Perhaps he was right, but the IPSA didn't last long enough to find out.

Fred Hemmings Jr. was at that meeting and signed a letter of intent. The '68 World Champion had recently counterpointed Scott's *Surfer* article with one called "Professionalism Is White!" Wrote Hemmings: "Professional surfing will identify our sport, improve all facets of competition, project a clean, healthy image, and vastly improve and regulate the advancement of surfing techniques." Fred put his weight behind developing something he called the Professional Surfing Association. He knew there was a vacuum, that competition was at the heart of male psychology, and that without it no one who didn't surf would ever have much interest in surfing.

Monumental snap-back by Tom Carroll, two-time World Champ from Australia, on the way to winning his third Pipeline Masters title in 1991; total prize money for the contest was $100,000.

The Bronzed Aussies

As it happened, the road to a successful world pro surfing tour was rocky at best. In the hiatus of the early '70s, a couple of attempts were made at a new kind of surfing event called an "Expression Session" at Pipeline. While interesting with some aesthetic highlights, the concept lacked a sense of purpose and clear goals; the masses wouldn't understand.

Then in 1972, the sixth World Contest (if you count the '64 in Oz, as surfers sometimes refer to Australia) was held in San Diego. The anticipated rematch between David Nuuhiwa and Nat Young never occurred since Nat had retired "back to the land" up at Byron Bay. Hemmings didn't bother to come either, since he knew he didn't have a prayer in small California surf. Nor did Rolf Aurness show up to defend his crown.

Nuuhiwa surfed brilliantly, the longboard nose-rider king having completely reinvented himself as a shortboard surfer, but the political winds seemed to be blowing another way, and there were rumblings from the local hoi polloi, too. His favorite board (a "Fish" design) was stolen, snapped in two, stabbed with a large kitchen knife, and hung in effigy from the Ocean Beach pier with a "GOOD LUCK DAVE" message scrawled on it. Apparently the locals at nearby Sunset Cliffs, who had developed the twin-tailed Fish, were feeling a tad proprietary. On a borrowed board, Nuuhiwa outclassed the competition but lost the event. "I want to get drunk and forget about it," he said afterward. Such are the vagaries of judging a kinetic artform. In the contest's dispirited aftermath, the International Surfing Federation and its World Contest dissolved into a dew.

Four years later, in September 1976, at the height of the new Aussie push, the International Professional Surfers (IPS) was founded by Hemmings for the expressed purpose of presenting the clean, healthy sport of surfing to a mainstream audience. By retroactively recognizing existing events around the world, the IPS instantly created the "pro tour" that Van Dyke

Founded by surfwear company Ocean Pacific in 1982, the annual Op Pro contest in Huntington Beach grew to become the largest American surfing contest, providing a scintillating showcase for the world's top surf talent. After his heat, the sands and stands crowded with thousands of spectators, future World Champ Sonny Garcia prepares to enter the gauntlet.

An attempt to organize an independent surf team and market it worldwide as an entity with commercial value was attempted in 1976 by a trio of Australian professional surfers. Galvanized by Sydney journalist Mike Hurst and calling themselves The Bronzed Aussies, Ian Cairns, Peter Townend, and Mark Warren packaged themselves as a

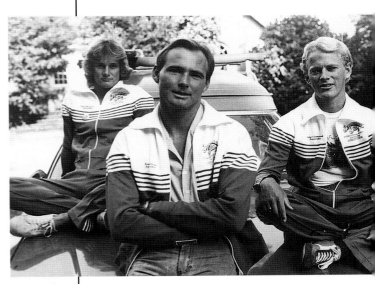

Much of professional surfing's development in the latter half of the 20th century was the doing of two of the three founding Bronzed Aussies, Ian Cairns (center) and Peter Townend (right).

new style of professional surf team futuristically geared to emerging consumer marketing trends. Stylistically and fashion-wise, however, the boys looked way too square for the times.

A fourth member, young Cheyne Horan, soon joined the team, and when Mark Warren bailed in 1978, Jim Banks became the fifth surfer to wear the distinctive matching competition sweats. The Bronzed Aussies had considerably more success in memory than they enjoyed at the time of their partnership. The idea of a similar group called the Sons of Hawaii was briefly attempted in the Islands.

and Sorrell had visualized. Having been involved in preliminary discussions with executives of a company called Beachcomber Bill's, who were willing to invest in a 1977 Grand Prix of Surfing, Peter Townend and his Bronzed Aussies buddy, Western Australian hottie Ian Cairns, buzzed around the world surfing in every money event they could find. So when the points were added up at year's end—*voila!*—Townend, an excellent all-around surfer, was surfing's first professional world champion (without winning a contest all year), and Cairns finished second. In a brief ceremony staged for a Honolulu newspaper photographer at the Outrigger Canoe Club, Hemmings snatched a gold-cup trophy from a shelf and presented it to a beaming Townend, then replaced it on the shelf.

It was a great gamble. Professional surfing had a tour (and a legal way for a few talented individuals to make money), just like golf and tennis. The purse for the 1977 tour was already $146,000, and pro surfing—despite some ups and downs—never looked back. After a falling-out with Hemmings, Cairns campaigned for a new concept—the Association of Surfing Professionals—on a platform of self-rule in November-December of 1982. In a bloodless coup, the IPS and Hemmings fell, and the ASP (supported by dollars from Ocean Pacific, one of the most successful surfwear companies) took control of the pro tour.

Curiously, the first five world surfing champions (winning nine world titles) of the pro era were from the Southern Hemisphere, and four (winning eight of those titles) were from Australia (Townend, Rabbit, the phenomenal Mark Richards, and Tom Carroll). Richards (a.k.a. MR) won four, Carroll two, and Shaun Tomson from South Africa one.

Four-time World Champ Mark Richards and his trusty twin-fin surfboard, photographed in Hollywood by Norman Seef for the cover of Surfing *magazine, while Simon Anderson was busy adding that extra fin.*

Next Generation Curren

The California-born son of notorious big-wave surfer Pat Curren, Tom Curren quietly and methodically surfed his way up the amateur ranks as pro surfing was coalescing. A Christian lad of prodigious abilities, he twice turned down contest winnings to be able to surf in (and win) the resurrected (and still amateur) World Championship in Australia in 1982. Curren was signed by Ocean Pacific and advertised into the best-known surfer of his generation, even before winning his first World title in 1986. He won again in '87, married and retired to France for a couple of years, then came back to the Pro Tour to win again in 1990.

Tom Curren has been the subject of extensive media interest and was profiled by *Rolling Stone* magazine. He was bold in his personal boycotting of South African surfing events during the apartheid era, dared to surf without sponsor logos on his board, and preferred playing music (guitar) to being interviewed. Since retiring from competition in the early '90s, he's remained a quiet and respected presence in the sport and continues to be a revered stylist, traveling the world in search of perfect waves.

Three-time World Champ Tom Curren cuts back to set up a tube ride at Off the Wall, a spot often referred to as Kodak Reef because it's such a perfect setup. Above: Tom with his father, North Shore legend Pat Curren.

Surfing as Art

To some, riding waves is a religion. To others it's a sport—good healthy exercise and, they claim, nothing more. Some have said it's an ephemeral and transient art form. If surfing is an art, perhaps it's a martial art, but in the spirit of *aikido*, the art of peace, one that uses the opponent's own force to overcome.

"When an opponent comes forward, move in and greet him; if he wants to pull back, send him on his way." —Ueshiba, Morihei. *The Art of Peace, 1883–1969.*

This is the action of a man carving a surfboard on a wave. The wave tightens into a fist of power, the surfer moves into the barrel to greet it. The muscle relaxes, the fist opens and pulls back, the surfer slams off the wide-open face of the wave, laying the shoreward rail of his board into a clean arc of beatific contempt.

From the perspective of the artist surfer, it's a beautiful thing.

"The aim of *aikido* is to harmonize with the opponent in a dance that calmly harnesses and redirects the force of the opponent for one's own purposes," says waterman and *aikido* master Carlisle Landel. "In *aikido*, we are taught to 'blend' or harmonize with our opponent, so that we enter a dance in which we calmly harness and redirect the forces of the opponent for our own purposes.

"In surfing, some see the ocean as an opponent that, like a mugger, is out to get us. But the true surfer calmly harmonizes with the wave, harnessing and redirecting the forces of mother ocean in a dance of breathtaking beauty.

"Both arts require balance and finesse, and attention to the calm center in the midst of chaos."

The art of the dance, as personified in Gerry Lopez at the Pipeline on Oahu's North Shore. Poise, style, grace under pressure—these forms of expression are the name of the game in surfing.

While 20th-century surfing has been primarily a male sport, there have always been excellent women surfers. The fabulous Calhouns—easy on the eyes, terrific in the waves—Robyn, Marge, and Candy at Makaha in 1962. Marge, the mother, was married to Hevs McClelland, American surfing's great funnyman, who was featured in several of Bud Browne's films. Right: Four-time Women's World Champ Margo Godfrey rides the nose at Hammonds Reef in 1967, the year before she won her first title in Puerto Rico. The poster (above right) is indicative of the extraordinary growth in women's surfing in the 1990s.

< Surfing Wahines >

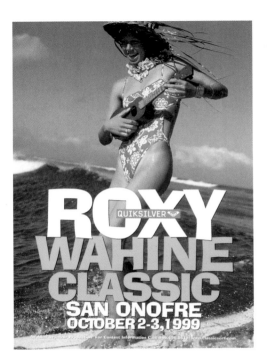

Prior to European contact, most everyone in Hawaii rode waves—men, women, and children; common people and royalty—but in the cultural twilight of the late-nineteenth and early-twentieth centuries, female surfers were not a fixture on the beaches of Waikiki, except for the tourists being entertained by beach boys on their large tandem surfboards. While a few women rode surfboards as early as the 1920s, into the '90s surfing remained a predominantly male sport. During the '50s and '60s, macho misogynist bad-boy behavior was elevated to the ranks of tribal ritual; from the days of North Shore "barracks" hell-dates and Narrabeen clubhouse gang bangs to 1980s pro-circuit headbanger excess and "carnal-val" atmosphere, women were virtually excluded from the inner circle of the sport.

Historically, this exclusion was partly a function of the size and weight of the equipment, but after a while it became a cultural mindset, a men's club sort of thing. Even so, there were a few stellar water-women in the pre–World War II years, notably Mary Ann Hawkins, the first California female surf hero. Thanks to lighter, more maneuverable equipment (courtesy of Joe Quigg and others), women started surfing at Malibu in the postwar years. One of them, Vicky Flaxman, was on that momentous trip to Windansea with the first potato chip boards in 1950 and surfed the outside peak all the way to the beach, getting a big round of applause from the guys.

The following decades brought a succession of outstanding women surfers and milestones, including

Margo Godfrey Oberg went on to raise a family, working as a surf instructor at a Kauai resort, pioneering a lifetime path for other professional women surfers.

Makaha champions Ethel Kukea, Vicky Heldrich, Nancy Nelson, and Marge Calhoun. A crescendo of sorts was reached in the early 1960s when a handful of talented young ladies vied for top honors in the newly formed USSA. Linda Benson (who, in 1963 at age fifteen, became the first woman to surf Waimea Bay), Phyllis O'Donnell, Joey Hamasaki, Nancy Nelson, the great Joyce Hoffman, and East Coaster Mimi Monroe were the shining stars of the amateur world, receiving polite applause from officials but generally ignored. Hoffman, the most successful competitor of the 1960s, won plenty of trophies, perks, and press, but never a living wage.

The first crack in this picture appeared in 1967, when four women—Joyce Hoffman, Joey Hamasaki, Margo Godfrey, and Cathy Lienhard—were included in the Western Surfing Association's new AAAA division for "professionally-oriented super stars." The youngest of them, Godfrey, would go on to become one of the greatest surfing champions, winning the World Title at age fifteen, then earning a place in the lineup at Sunset Beach and other big-wave spots. In the late '60s, Sharron Weber, Lynn Boyer, and Martha Sunn were also at the top of their games, but the path of the female pro surfer was paved by Margo Godfrey (later Margo Godfrey Oberg), who parlayed her World Championship wins in 1968, '77, '80, and '81 into a lifestyle career as a teaching pro on Kauai.

In 1980, the men's World Tour prize money had risen to $243,850, while the women's purses totaled $10,000, a historic low. That year, at the OM-Bali Pro contest in good waves at Uluwatu, Linda Davoli of New Jersey became the first woman to surf one-on-one against a man, losing to Australian Stuart Campbell by a respectable 74 to 60.5, but well out of the money. It was a step, however, and soon women surfers began to be perceived as athletes of real stature in the sport.

California-born Rochelle Ballard has been a touring pro for well over a decade. Married to filmmaker Bill Ballard, living on the North Shore allowed her to develop trademark moves like this solid cutback; she's well known for charging big waves with the best of them.

Right: Surfing Girl was just one of several magazines targeting female surfers that emerged in the 1990s.

In the '80s and '90s, a new generation of explosive female surfers, aided and abetted by the thruster-style surfboards, literally slashed onto the scene. They were led by powerful surfers like Santa Barbara's Kim Mearig and Florida's Frieda Zamba, women who ripped strong slash-backs and with lip-smacks that were damn near as potent as the men's. Along with Australia's Pam Burridge and Pauline Menczer and South Africa's Wendy Botha, they drove a clear wedge between the past and the future. Thanks to them, women's surfing turned a corner in the 1980s. Prize money for the women, a pauper's feast at the start of the decade, grew at a faster pace than the men is and had climbed past the quarter-million-dollar mark by 1990.

Into this new world charged Lisa Andersen, a runaway from Ormond Beach, Florida, who would capture the World Title four times in the 1990s. Virtually homeless when she arrived in California, Andersen surfed every morning, waited tables part-time, and honed her skills in the competition-rich National Scholastic Surfing Association (created by former Bronzed Aussies Ian Cairns and Peter

(continued on p. 156)

Lisa Andersen

In an article in *Outside* magazine titled "Gidget Kicks Ass" (November 1996), Martha Sherrill wrote: "Within the anachronistically macho world of surfing, respect comes when you rip like a man and act like it's no big thing. Two-time world champion Lisa Andersen is the first woman to pull this off, changing the way beach boys look at beach girls and bringing droves of young women to the sport."

At twenty-eight, Andersen toured the world with her four-year-old daughter, Erica, winning her fourth straight World Title in 1997. Two summers before, she had competed in a specialty event on the men's World Championship Tour called the Quiksilver Pro; she was one of four women invited to join the forty-eight men in the jungle at the remote and dangerous G-Land event site, and she earned considerable respect from the male athletes by going for it in the big, grinding barrels, getting her face made over on the reef in the process.

Since surfing is such a male-dominated sport, for a woman to become a competent surfer is a real achievement, and to become a great one is rare indeed. Certainly, the short, light, thruster-style surfboard has made it easier for women (and kids) to get into surfing. "A longboard is something you retire to," says Andersen. The thrusters are "a lot easier and a lot looser, more maneuverable. Some women have small frames, and they don't like to carry around a longboard."

When she ran away from her Florida home at sixteen, Andersen left her mother a note that said she was going to be the number-one surfer in the world. She went to Huntington Beach, California, where former pro surfer and coach Ian Cairns found her sleeping under a table in at the beach one morning. When she woke up, she begged for a slot in the National Scholastic Surfing Association contest Ian was running, and he let her in without the requisite parental consent or student ID. Of course, she won the event, and the rest is hunger, hard work, and history.

Lisa Andersen came out of Ormond Beach, Florida, to become the dominant female surfer of the 1990s. At times traveling to international events with her infant daughter, she demonstrated a range of skills and a focused determination that put her on an equal footing with top female athletes in sports like tennis, track, and golf. As a lifestyle iconoclast, she incited an explosive growth in women's surfing and female beach fashion as the face of Quiksilver's Roxy brand.

Townend). She collected thirty-five trophies in one eight-month stretch, culminating in the U.S. Amateur Championship near her home at Sebastian Inlet in 1987. She immediately turned pro and, despite her short season, ended the year twelfth-ranked in the world and was named ASP Women's Rookie of the Year.

Andersen's dominance of women's pro surfing in the 1990s was profound, as she went on to equal the 4-time-world-champion marks reached by fellow Floridian Frieda Zamba ('84, '85, '86, '88), South African Wendy Botha ('87, '89, '91, '92), and the illustrious groundbreaker herself, Margo Godfrey Oberg ('68, '77, '80, '81). But Andersen achieved her four titles in successive years.

Something about Lisa Andersen fired imaginations—men's to some extent, but mostly women and younger girls, looking for some direction. Her sheer charisma seemed to lend cultural significance to everything she did. Sponsored in the'90s by Quiksilver's new women's company, Roxy, Andersen's preference for a man's-style surf trunk was arguably the key influence in launching a billion-dollar fashion movement.

Through the vehicle of surfing, in a few short years, Lisa Andersen transformed her life, achieving goals only she once thought were possible. Women's surfing didn't stand still, however—not any more. No sooner did Andersen step aside to concentrate on raising children than Australian Layne Beachley (living on the North Shore) proceeded to rip off four straight World Titles herself. Meanwhile, twenty years from its nadir, the boom in women's surfing was side by side with giant-wave tow-in surfing as the biggest phenomenon to shake up the sport since the shortboard revolution of the 1960s.

< New School and Beyond >

Surfing performance soared, literally, to new heights as aerial and skateboard-style maneuvers pioneered by '70s skate-surf icon Larry Bertlemann merged with the extraordinary carving abilities of the thruster surfboards to create an increasingly radical approach to wave-riding. The pace of the action mounted steadily through the 1980s, as champions like South African Martin Potter, Aussie Mark Occhilupo, and Californian Tom Curren steadily pushed the envelope. It all culminated in '90s' so-called New School surfing, a new generation of rising stars with repertoires inspired by skateboard and snowboard maneuvers. Throwing big airs, side-slipping, fishtailing, and skating across the tops of tubes, the young pack included Rob Machado, Kalani Robb, Keith and Chris Malloy, Ross Williams, Shane Beschen, Taylor Knox, Corey Lopez, and a score of other progressive surfers. Much of their fire was spread around the world via the lens of San Diego—area videographer Taylor Steele.

The appetite for these videos (and those of a hundred imitators) was huge, and new performance territory carved out by these dynamic young surfers was amplified worldwide with unprecedented speed. As yet another generation (with the most aggressive style yet) entered the lineups at thousands of surf spots, the face of surfing was once again transformed and, in the opening years of the third millennium, the sport was truly light years away from where it had been a mere one hundred years before.

From grommets to surf stars: Who could have predicted (back in 1987 when the photo was taken) that one of these hot little surfers would become the most successful professional surfer of all time? Left to right: Mattie Liu, Sean Slater, Walt Cerney, Shane Dorian, and Kelly Slater.

Meanwhile, a longboard renaissance also gained ground in the mid-'80s as numerous surf stars and baby-boomers turned forty and the easier paddling characteristics of the big sticks gained renewed appeal, not to mention a nostalgia for more uncrowded times. Energized by charismatic longboard stylists like Jonathan Paskowitz, Herbie Fletcher, and (ironically) shortboard pioneer Nat Young, the ASP instituted a longboard world championship in 1988. Here was an interesting meeting place of old school and new, of older surfer and younger. A key philosophical issue was addressed with the initial rules for judging: longboard surfing was not shortboard surfing on big boards, it was something inherently different, involving grace and style and especially movement up and down the board. Once again, longboard surfing was represented at the highest professional levels of the sport, Nat Young (and his son Beau, too, in 2000) was a world champ (four times in the '80s and '90s), and conflict between shortboarders and longboarders became a worldwide territorial issue.

157

No other surfer of the modern era has so thoroughly dominated professional surfing as has Florida's Kelly Slater. Proving himself in big Waimea at the 1996 Eddie (right) was par for the course for this six-time World Champ. Above: Out of the water and into the arms of adoring fans, celeb Slater wades to the beach following a Huntington Beach session during the 1995 Op Pro.

Kelly Slater

Kelly Slater was another order of phenomenon. From humble Florida origins, a torrid amateur surfing career in high school, and a meteoric rise to World Champion, Quiksilver's $1 million-a-year kid reigned supreme in the 1990s, in a way that has rarely occurred in the history of the sport. With spectacular good looks, shy intelligence, fearless abandon, and a relentless need to win, he became a subject of fascination far beyond the limits of surf culture. Costar of the rave TV show *Baywatch* for a couple of seasons, cover boy on *Interview* magazine in '95, and featured in *People* magazine's "50 Most Beautiful People" issue, Slater seemed to be unabashedly trying to get as much out of surfing as he could without prostituting himself.

Born in Cocoa Beach, Florida, Kelly Slater was one of the wave of "new school" surfers who led a worldwide shift in surfing performance and style in the 1990s. He rose to prominence as the 1986 U.S. Surfing Champion, then won his first professional event (and $30,600) in 1990. By 1992, at age twenty, he was the youngest world champ ever. After a slack year in '93, he reemerged as a futuristic wunderkind, reinventing surfing and blowing away all opposition. He proceeded to win five consecutive World Titles before taking a three-year sabbatical from the tour. The sabbatical began with a fifth Pipeline Masters title for the seeming superhero.

After a lengthy and well-publicized relationship with former *Baywatch* and home-video star Pamela Anderson, Slater joined the best big-wave surfers in the world at Waimea Bay in January of 2001. He took fifth place, and then returned the following year to win the event.

Meanwhile, specialty Masters events were added to the ASP program, converging the stars of previous generations at good surf spots in interesting parts of the world on an annual or semiannual basis. Although the "old pros" weren't making the kind of money the kids were scoring on their blade-thin thrusters, at the 1997 Rip Curl/Surf Dive 'n' Ski Super Skins, held at Bells Beach in Australia, Mark Occhilupo (a remarkable, moody talent with a blue-collar ethic) walked off with $55,000 in cash and a $30,000 Jeep.

The ASP World Tour (both men's and women's) gained considerable momentum throughout the 1990s, its annual prize-money offering rising into the millions of dollars. The year 2002

It is ironic that Nat Young, who sounded the death knell of the noseriding era and spearheaded the shortboard revolution, should have been a central inspiration in the creation of the ASP's world longboard circuit. Now a four-time World Longboard Champion, Nat exemplifies the surfer as waterman, with a wide range of skills and the ability to use the appropriate vehicle for the conditions. And sometimes that means a big surfboard!

found former "backside attack" charger Rabbit Bartholomew installed as president and CEO of ASP International, administering a two-tiered ratings system, incorporating the Top 44, who automatically qualified for the World Championship Tour, and the World Qualifying Series (WQS) functioning as a global feeder system for the WCT.

In the mid-'90s, a major shift of philosophy moved the majority of WCT events from highly urbanized surf centers to grade-A surf spots, no matter how remote, relying on improved global communications technology (like real-time streaming on the internet) for media impact. Thus the tour included competition in exotic locales in Australia, Tahiti, Fiji, South Africa, Portugal, France, Brazil, and Hawaii, sponsored by large surf and mainstream companies anxious to ride the great planet surf wave. Augmented by pro women's, juniors', and longboard tours, and underpinned by numerous national pro and amateur tours (as well as regional and local contests, too), competitive surfing was alive and well in 2002.

In 2002, both Slater and Lisa Andersen returned to the World Championship Tour, receiving full-season wildcard entries in their respective WCT divisions—Slater going for a seventh men's title, Andersen for a women's fifth. So recently surfing's precocious teen wonder, Slater, now thirty and mounting his comeback after three years off the tour, was hoping to prove that surfing was not just a young man's sport.

<The Green Soul of Surfing>

Environmental awareness had been growing within the surfing population since Honolulu surfer John Kelly created Save Our Surf (SOS) to save the beaches of Waikiki in 1961. In California, the unsuccessful fight to save Dana Point from the Army Corps of Engineers (ACE) further galvanized surfers in the mid-'60s. For longtime surfers, the giant breakwall is a painful reminder of the glory days of "Killer Dana," one of California's early big-wave spots. By the end of the decade, surfers were becoming proactive over issues like beach access, oil spills, proposed harbors, coastal development, and the pollution of ocean waters.

One of the first things surfer/shaper Steve Pezman did when he became editor of *Surfer* in 1970 was to establish a new magazine department, "OMO" (for Our Mother Ocean), a forum for environmental issues. Replacing John Severson as the magazine's publisher in 1971, Pezman's persistence began to bear fruit, albeit indirectly, in the late '70s and early '80s when a number of surfers became more active in their communities and environments.

In the late '70s, three Northern California surfers observed a local fisherman removing rocks from one of the reefs that produced the excellent waves at Shelter Cove and using them to build a breakwater to shelter his boats. One of the surfers, Tom Pratte, was an environmental studies major at Cal State Humboldt; Pratte embraced the "deep ecology" philosophy that underpinned radical environmental organizations like Earth First! and the Sea Shepherd Society. After trying various forms of friendly persuasion, then rousing public opinion against this illegal destruction of a natural reef area, Pratte was able to get the California Coastal Commission involved and, finally, stopped the breakwater. After several years of solo campaigning on this and other issues, Pratte landed a job as "the environmental guy" with the Western Surfing Association and moved his focus to stop ACE drainage of Malibu Lagoon, which was destroying the surf break and polluting Santa Monica Bay. With persistence and keen research skills, Pratte won a $3,000 grant from the WSA and ongoing support from foam magnate Grubby Clark, which he used to make considerable headway in a number of areas, notably where ACE projects threatened coastal wetlands and surf spots. His efforts paved the way for the creation of the Surfrider Foundation and other surfing-related environmental organizations.

Surfrider Foundation cofounders Glenn Hening (top) and Tom Pratte (1949–1994). Nobody is in a better position to assess the quality of the near-shore environment than a surfer.

Because surfing involves such intimate contact with the natural world at a time when most humans are increasingly sealed off in artificial surroundings, surfers have some responsibility for alerting others about any problems they become aware of in the ocean environment. As Bill Hamilton wrote in 1971, "Just by the fact that we ride the waves of the ocean, we are major responsibility holders to the future and ecology of earth."

Former world champ Nat Young was quite vocal on environmental issues and even ran for Australian state parliament on an environmental platform: "With such a large number of surfers on the planet, I think we should be speaking from an environmental platform because that is where we're coming from," he said in a 1996 interview. "Longboarders, shortboarders, all of these people that add up to being members of this big tribe called surfing, we're all saying that *these* should be your priorities—number one, environment!"

Following the impetus of Surfrider, numerous other surf-based environmental organizations emerged around the world, including Surfers Against Sewage in England, the Surfers Environmental Alliance in California, and Groundswell Society, created by Surfrider cofounder Glenn Hening, "For the sake of tending the soul in surfing." The spirit behind all of this was Tom Blake's "God = Nature" all over again.

<The Surfrider Foundation>

Glenn Hening, a surfer and a computer specialist at Jet Propulsion Laboratory in Pasadena, wanted to create an organization that would give surfers a way to get involved in their communities. He hooked up with Lance Carson ("the most famous surfer I knew"), who was vitally concerned about Malibu and knew Tom Pratte. This led to a three-way conversation that prompted Hening, in 1984, to found the Surfrider Foundation, surfing's first nonprofit environmental organization. Pratte served on the board of directors and later as Surfrider's executive director.

With financial support from Grubby Clark and founding members like Yvon Chouinard at Patagonia, Inc. (who donated $10,000 for artificial-reef development and some $65,000 overall in Surfrider's first decade), plus help from the surfing magazines (which ran free membership ads), Surfrider quickly became a presence in the surfing community. "Tom Pratte played a key role in establishing our credibility with his environmental research," says Hening, who left the group in '86. "I was like the booster rocket," he jokes. Hening continues to be involved in clean-water efforts and publishes the *Ground Swell Society* annual.

When Eddie Vedder (top left) of Pearl Jam donated $50,000 to the Surfrider Foundation, he did it in front of a toilet because, he said, "that's what the oceans are turning into." Surfrider's MOM (Music for Our Mother Ocean) album showed broad-based support in the music world for protecting water quality in the surfing world. By the end of 2002, two more albums had been added to the series.

During Pratte's tenure, Surfrider joined San Francisco attorney Mark Massara in bringing suit against two Humboldt County pulp mills that were polluting Northern California surfing areas. Surfrider was in turn joined by the EPA (there were over 40,000 documented violations of the Clean Water Act at the mills, operated by Louisiana Pacific and Simpson Paper Co.) and won its case in 1991, the second largest CWA suit in American history. "The paper mills tried to buy Surfrider off," Hening says. "'How much money for this to go away?' they asked us. We told 'em, 'We want clean water,' and they said, 'Sure, that's cute, but really, what will it take for this to go away?' And we said, 'We want clean water.'"

This and other successes (blocking breakwaters at Bolsa Chica, Seal Beach, and Imperial Beach in California, restoring natural dunes habitat on the Outer Banks in North Carolina, winning mitigation and an artificial reef at a Standard Oil plant in El Segundo, California, and saving the surf at Big Cove at Sandy Hook, New Jersey) brought a lot of attention to Surfrider, which in turn attracted many non-surfers to its board and staff and garnered other forms of support.

In 1991, on behalf of Surfrider International, Tom Curren organized a large and effective protest paddle down the Adour River to its mouth, which spills into the Bay of Biscay at the infamous surf spot, Le Barre (infamous because it's been destroyed by jetties). The river, said Curren, "is infested with the whole spectrum of pollution—heavy metals, chemicals, and bacteria. Our paddle was to demonstrate that we're very concerned with the quality of water we're surfing in." Since this action, the government has stepped in and forced industry and agriculture to clean up their acts.

In 1995, surfer Eddie Vedder and his band Pearl Jam donated $50,000 to Surfrider "for their work to protect the oceans." John Densmore of The Doors donated $15,000, and the organization's many "in kind" contributors include *Rolling Stone* magazine and MTV (both at $50,000), the Surf Industries Manufacturing Association (SIMA), Interscope Records and Surfdog Records (at $100,000), *Wired* magazine, and a slew of other surfing and nonsurfing businesses and individuals. Its advisory board includes Patagonia's Chouinard, actors Woody Harrelson and Gregory Harrison, the Beach Boys, and Mati Waiya of the Chumash people, native inhabitants of the Malibu coast.

In 1996, Surfrider and Surfdog Records teamed up on a CD project called *MOM (Music for Our Mother Ocean),* which included gifted original songs by such illustrious music makers as Beastie Boys, Jewel, No Doubt, Porno For Pyros, Pearl Jam, and others and raised over $200,000 for the organization. A second MOM effort featured Dick Dale's "Miserlou '97" ("Metallica meets Dick Dale," according to former executive director Pierce Flynn); *MOM III* was released in 2000 and featured Paul McCartney, Beck, Ben Harper, Red Hot Chili Peppers, and other great bands.

By 2002, Surfrider, "a grassroots-based non-profit environmental organization," had over 30,000 members in fifty chapters in the United States and Puerto Rico, plus affiliates in Australia, Brazil, Europe, and Japan.

< Surfwear & Culture Shock >

Surf fashion began when the first surfers who traveled to Hawaii adopted the casual apparel of the tropics—aloha shirts, Hawaiian-style trunks, beach sandals—then returning home, where such apparel was, by definition, exotic. Actually, from a California or mainland standpoint, surfing itself was exotic. It was certainly an unusual sight in the pre–World War II years, then in the '50s and '60s it acclimatized in California, but only sort of. Surfing always takes place "abroad"—in the boundary-less sea—and its cultural life is on the beach, that desert of ionized silicon dioxide, that no-man's-land where people strip naked and just lay around and relax. It's all pretty exotic, and so is the culture that emerges, almost by definition. And that's what gives surfing its allure and surfwear its cachet.

From its humble beginnings in the hand-painted or stenciled *tapa* (bark) cloth garments of the early 1900s (actually a synthesis of the American pioneers' Thousand Mile Shirt and a Japanese work shirt called a *palaka* in the Islands) to the silk, cotton, and rayon (invented by DuPont in '24) aloha shirts created for tourists in the '20s and '30s, the Hawaiian shirt spear-

By the 1940s, the "aloha" shirt was almost a Hawaiian icon, along with lei and ukelele. President Harry Truman proudly wore a humidity-creased aloha shirt on the cover of Life (left). A curious side note: Hawaiian print artist Keoni (John Miggs) designed a "surfboard for kiddies" in 1950, a four-and-a-half-foot-long wooden "Hawaiian Surfboard"—as he called it—with rollerskate wheels attached!

Something there is in surfing that so perfectly fuses peace and danger, leisure and dramatic physicality, artful dance and contorted pratfall, that the sport conjures the creative, the whimsical, the kooky like no other. Above: Rick Rietveld's interpolation of Einstein into the Elvis Blue Hawaii concept was witty and wonderful.

164

headed the Polynesian surf-style invasion of staid European-inspired mainland attire. Inspired by the *palaka* and silk shirts his Punahou classmates wore (made from kimono fabric), Ellery J. Chun created the first aloha shirts in 1931. His designs were made by Wong's Products in Honolulu and sold through his family's King-Smith Clothiers for about a dollar each. In 1936, Chun introduced the "Aloha Shirt" label, and the term and the style caught on with beach boys and surfers. When the concept was meshed with the exquisite floral designs of Musa-Shiya (the Shirtmaker of Shoten), Elsie Das (Hawaiian Originals), John Miggs (a.k.a. Keoni of Hawaii), and others, an industry was born.

Kamehameha Garment Company, Ltd. (founded by Herbert and Millie Briner) and Branfleet (founded by George Brangier and Nat Norfleet and later called Kahala) were the first to incorporate. Kahala's "pineapple tweeds" shirt was extremely popular in the '30s. Bearing the Royal Hawaiian crest and the motto, "The life of the land is perpetuated in righteousness," the shirt was worn and endorsed by Duke Kahanamoku, for which he received a fifty-cents-per-unit royalty, making him the first surfer sponsored by a sportswear company. The shirts were casually popularized by celebrities who wore them—Hollywood surfers Richard Boone and Peter Lawford at Waikiki with the Duke in '47, Harry Truman on a 1951 cover of *Life*, Montgomery Clift in 1953's *From Here to Eternity*, Arthur Godfrey on his mid-'50s TV show (he wore a new one every day), and Elvis in *Blue Hawaii* in '63.

Hawaiian shirts became the basis of the surfer look and were—along with the tailored M. Nii surfing trunks of the '50s—the foundation on which today's multibillion-dollar surfwear industry was constructed. This surfer style had a burst of mainstream popularity in the early '60s, was eclipsed by the even louder statements of the psychedelic era, and looked corny in the conservative backlash of the '70s when, especially in California, surfers took on the organic neutrality of seals or dolphins, wearing black rubber suits and surfing plain, simple surfboards. But this couldn't last long because so much of surfing wasn't just surfing, it was style, and style (to some minds) means fashion.

In the late 1980s, surfing came back into mainstream consciousness with a vengeance, blasting into style across America and the world like never before. In fact, it was the planetary convergence of *three* board sports (surfing, skateboarding, and the rising star of snowboarding) that magnified the impact, creating a powerful nexus of radical image, insouciant attitude, and contemporary street art that caught America's youth in midstride and swept them to the beach on the shifting winds of fashion. Sitting fat and happy and ready to reap the rewards, the established surfwear companies were feeling cocky. "If you don't surf, don't start," imperiously suggested the first page of a Gotcha ad. "If you surf, never stop," advised the second. "Wave Attack!" "Surf Till It Hurts!" "Future Shock!" screamed the ads. Suddenly a California actor was in the White House and everybody wanted to be a punk surfer.

Whitey Harrison's granddaughter, Coco, led the retro scene as surfing flashed hot in the late 1980s and early '90s. The release of Bill Delaney's film Surfers for Gotcha Sportswear *heralded a new maturity in the medium. Meanwhile, when called upon, an ageless Mickey Muñoz would slip his veteran feet into his formal thongs.*

While the surfwear labels that survived the '70s and early '80s ramped up for the long-awaited payoff, a rash of new companies jumped into the scene, each trying to "out core" the other with "authentic" phrases, looks, and poses, and surf magazines swelled in size to well over two hundred pages. As top surf brands were snapped up by the big, prestigious department stores, product poured into the mass market like never before. Kids all over the country (and soon the world) were wearing Gotcha, Stüssy, Rusty, Quiksilver, and Life's A Beach. Seizing the moment (as good surfers have been trained to do), dozens of surfboard manufacturers (skate and snow companies, too) hustled to shift their emphasis from hard goods to soft goods (clothes) in time to capitalize on the boom.

"Surfing Is Life, The Rest Is Details," summarized one ad for Instinct, and the rest of the world was starting to get the metaphor. The crush for retail space was mind-boggling—Jimmy'Z, Billabong, Surf Fetish, Cruz, Pure Juice, Spot Sport European Beach, No Fear, Airwalk, Kozmik, Town & Country, Ooh Mau Mao, Maui and Sons, Local Motion, Mossimo, Island Magic, Island Scene, Hawaiian Island Creations, Bad Boyz, Local Boy'z, Newport Blue, Gordon & Smith, Body Glove, O'Neill, yet another reincarnation of Hang Ten . . . suddenly there were literally thousands of surfwear companies in the world.

In 1990, Bill *Free Ride* Delaney's new film, *Surfers: The Movie* opened to an enthusiastic surf press. Designed "to bring back the phenomenon of the surf film," it didn't fulfill the mission conceived by producer Michael Tomson of Gotcha, largely because the surf-video market was just taking off. *Surfers* was certainly the right name, though, because surfers were now in demand everywhere. Hawaiian hunk Vince Klyn, weathering Aussie Nat Young, Ivy League–style islander Buzzy Kerbox, smoldering world champ Tom Curren, and a dozen other "typical" image surfers were sought after for prestigious fashion shoots in Hollywood, New York City, or on location.

< The Cult of Cool >

"Before the '40s the beach was a place to which the encumbered urban culture attempted to transport itself relatively intact. Then came the atomic age. California surfers of the '50s were the first to 'get naked,' grow their hair long and flip-off society—giving initial impetus to today's beach scene. . . . Unabashedly hedonistic and narcissistic, the beach culture is now truly a significant marketplace of the modern human condition. As the beach culture matures, it diversifies, incubating and spinning-off hybrid subcults that develop core followings, which in turn become assimilated back into the energy of the whole."

—Steve Pezman, publisher, in the first issue of *Beach Culture*, 1989.

Beach Culture, *the short-lived but far-reaching brainchild of designer David Carson, crystallized the graphic vocabulary of "board sports," paving the way for a plethora of surf-skate-snowboard magazines during the 1990s.*

Right: *A brash attitude, a ready grin, and a flashy repertoire tend to pay off . . . and they certainly have for the Fletcher clan (Christian, Herbie, Nathan, and Dibbee)—exemplars of beach culture.*

In a world where cool was becoming everything, surfing was now the cult of cool, and the commercial vampires wanted to get their teeth into its big, pulsing vein. The history, memorabilia, and paraphernalia of surfing were all in big demand. *The New Yorker* ran a huge two-part article on the life and times of San Francisco surfer Mark Renneker, a hardcore surfer, physician, and cofounder of the Surfer's Medical Association; it was a great stereotype-breaker. Meanwhile Christian Fletcher (head shaved, tattooed, and pierced) was short-circuiting the three top board sports into a new synthesis that would forever alter the subcultural character of each. In the middle of the late-'80s rush (and between sessions with photographer Bruce Weber for Ralph Lauren), Nat Young described the moment for *Surfing* magazine:

"Surfing has been put across as a cult and it is a cult. I've been on this tribal thing for a long time. As a tribe, surfers are all after something the normal man in the street doesn't have a bloody clue about. I mean, surfers are becoming respectable now, a lot of people have put a lot of effort into that and that's great. But we *know* we're into something different" [*Surfers,* November 1989].

Surfing was now pop culture in a big, big way, and it had pragmatically adjusted its own culture accordingly. The complex character that Rick Griffin's cartoon Murphy had become (innocent gremmie turned mystic peyote-droppin' seeker turned born-again Christian) was replaced in the pages of *Surfer* with the demographically low-pitched surf goon Wilbur Kookmeyer. The magazines (especially *Surfing*) adjusted their marketing to fit the target audience of the rag merchants—young males, twelve to eighteen—because they were the ones who spent the bucks. In 1989, *Surfer* launched *Beach Culture,* a magazine that celebrated the cutting edge of surfer style and its various influences and cross-pollinations.

Although the surf market sagged briefly in the early '90s, it quickly rebounded. Many of the small surf companies started by novice surf entrepreneurs in the 1970s were publicly-traded and no longer small. Quiksilver reported sales of over $600 million in 2001; Billabong (established in Australia in 1973) weighed in at over $280 million, and California-based Ocean Pacific (founded in 1972) reversed a backwards slide, storming back to $200 million.

In 2002, former Billabong licensee Bob Hurley, who spun off his own Hurley International board-sport brand in the late '90s, sold out to sportswear giant Nike, which was looking for an entrée into the lucrative youth/surf market. Both Hurley and Billabong were among dozens of companies now affluent enough to maintain a stable of team riders in an industry that in the United States alone was valued at over $4.5 billion in 2001.

Surf shops, too, had progressed far from their low-rent roots; the surf shops of the '80s and '90s were slick lifestyle operations selling sophisticated gear for full pop. But the boutiquing of surfing had been going on for decades. That old bar of Parawax that was good enough for traction in the '50s became Surf Research's Waxmate in the '60s, Dr. Zog's Sex Wax in the '70s, and Big Pecker Surf Wax by 1990, and by then most kids were applying AstroDeck or similar cushioned traction pads to the decks of their boards anyway. The beaver-tail jacket and long-john wetsuit of the early '60s had bloomed into

Human nature is a complex web of characteristics—drives and fears; virtues and vices. These are reflected in man's pursuits. In surfing, the phenomenon of localism mirrors a conflicting maze of territorial imperatives, which are generally dealt with out in the water. Left: Surfers on the North Shore are intent on establishing priority from the get-go. Above: Warning to non-locals at the Sunset Cliffs trailhead, San Diego.

a highly sophisticated rubber market with the o'riginal folks hell-bent on staying ahead of a determined pack of newer players. All the new suits were leagues ahead of the best just ten years ago—lighter, more flexible, warmer—making it easier to surf in them. Sunglasses, too, became a universe of its own, with giant Oakley one of many successes (and averaging over $100 a pair!).

The rising tide of surf culture sloshed over America and much of the rest of the world in the '90s like a big Southern-Hemi swell. The industry's marketing research authority, Board-Trac, estimated there were 2.42 million surfers in the U.S. in 2001, averaging twenty-one years old, and about 20 percent of them were females. With half a million surfboards and a greater number of wetsuits sold annually, surfing was clearly in a boom phase. Bruce Brown came out of cinematic retirement to create *Endless Summer II* (1994), which reflected the times in its bipolar stars, Pat O'Connell, a hot twenty-year-old shortboarder, and Robert "Wingnut" Weaver, a stylish twenty-six-year-old longboarder. Although as mystified over what surfing's all about after seeing the film as before, *Chicago Sun-Times* film critic Roger Ebert wrote: "The movie is wonderfully photographed. Right at the beginning, we see fabulous shots of waves and surfers. Some of the shots even go inside the 'barrel,' so we can see the wave curling over the head of the surfer. What a way to get stoked. These are terrific shots. We see them again, and again, and again. The operative word in the title is endless, not summer."

And he was right. It *was* endless. The waves just kept coming, and the secret was out—that most anyone could paddle out and catch a free ride. There was no turning back this tide. It would have its highs and its lows, but the roots of this sport and its culture had taken a firm hold in the energized coastal terrain, where daily exposure to zillions of sprung ions transformed dazed victims of contemporary lockstep society into healthy human beings with a historical legacy and a sparkle in their eyes.

< Big Money, Bigger Dollars >

The big money coming into the sport via the sportswear companies meant bigger money for sponsored surfers. It was a dream that had been pursued since the Bronzed Aussies and even before. Corky Carroll was writing "professional surfer" on his tax returns back in 1965, when he was on the Hobie team. But the most Carroll claims to have made was about $40,000 in 1968, when his was the most recognizable name in surfing (he still ranks high in recognition, thanks to his round of Bud Lite commercials in the '80s . . . and maybe for his *Surfer for President* album in 1980). Makaha and Duke champion Joey Cabell made a good pile of money, but that was as a cofounder of the Chart House Restaurants (he still owns the one at Ala Moana near

As surfing gained momentum through the '70s and '80s, the top dogs experimented with the power and new ways of having fun. Corky Carroll reinvented himself as a guitar-pickin', folk-song singin', Bud Lite drinkin' Surfer for President. Gerry Lopez became Chairman of the Board at Lightning Bolt . . . for a while. And then the crowds got ugly in Huntington Beach, burning a couple of cop cars at the '86 Op Pro. Surfing finally made headlines in L.A. It was a riot.

Waikiki). Although he was photographed on Sunset Boulevard by rock photographer Norman Seef for the cover of *Surfing* in 1979 and looked plenty flashy in his silver Porsche, Mark Richards never made anything close to what surfers were making in 2000. Chris Carter, who was a senior editor at *Surfing* in those days, made a fortune, too, but that was as the creator and producer of *The X-Files* and other television projects.

Today, however, the top surfers are doing better. Marquee performers can run a successful surfwear company a cool $250,000 each, a price that's not unreasonable, according to Gotcha Sportswear founder Michael Tomson. He told reporter Matt Warshaw, "My theory is that 50 percent of all advertising and promotions are a complete waste of money—but nobody knows which 50 percent" ("Green on Blue," *The Surfer's Journal,* Fall 1996).

The Power and the Shark

One of surfing's most pithy aphorisms: Waves are measured in increments of fear. The allure and danger of riding big surf is a defining dimension in surf culture. In general, the better a surfer becomes, the larger and more powerful and exciting the waves he seeks to ride. Eventually this takes a person very close to the edge of his physical abilities. A surfer may have all the knowledge and technique and strength to ride a thirty-foot wave, but what if he makes a mistake?

Death by drowning is an image and a possibility that always lives in the surfer's mind. You're far out to sea, you've lost your surfboard, there's nowhere to stand, and you're cold and deadly tired. You want to rest.

Of course, even when the waves are not life-threatening, even on those idyllic afternoons of small fun waves and perfect warm weather, there is always that remote possibility of an . . . encounter with . . . the landlord. The man in the gray suit.

Although there have only been about thirty-five shark attacks on surfers in California since 1970 (and only one of them fatal, at Asilomar near Monterey in 1981), the close calls come frequently enough to stimulate the topic in the minds of the imaginative. So this, then, is another defining dimension of surfing. What other athlete has to consider the very real possibility of being eaten alive on the playing field?

Watching a swell approach, seeing it lurch up over submarine reefs and rise up into a wild and dangerous colossus can be a frightening thing. But sitting out there with your feet dangling can be nerve-wracking too. Waiting for the beast at Waimea. Inset: From the Frog House wall in Newport.

Contemporary Core

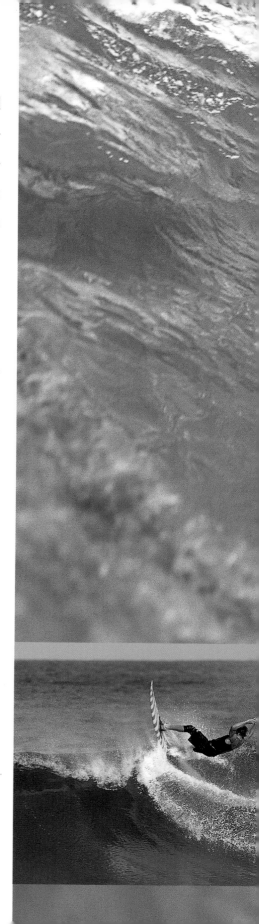

"And now it's a graying demographic that's become ready to look back and romanticize its youth. With all the collectibles and all this stuff now, it's definitely not a hula hoop—it's a market, an industry. It's a sport, it's on television, it's got a lingo that has changed with the eras, it's got a $5.5 million circuit, it's got books, it's got authors, it's got magazines—jeez!—it's got a history."
—Steve Pezman, publisher of *The Surfer's Journal,* 1997 interview

Surfing

is the ultimate metaphor for life. It accurately describes the way things happen. Life really is a wave, and your attitude is your surfboard. A situation—any opportunity—comes to you like a wave, and you are the surfer. You can't act before the situation develops, and you can't act after it passes. You can only act at the peak of the moment, where the energy is concentrated. You can play the metaphor at any level and, like surfing, with any style. You can surf with a hostile aggression or with a blank Zen mind. You can work at it and push yourself against your limits hour after hour, or you can make it a rich, sensual experience—the beautiful, luscious curling barrel-muscle inviting you to penetrate and work your stick around inside (that sort of thing). A wave is a clear slate and a living mirror. Beach culture is what's reflected off of it. Surf culture is stepping through the mirror.

When the cyberspace cadets started in with their "surfing the web" stuff, the collective unconscious was unlocked in some big way. Suddenly it's clear that everybody in the world (virtually) wants to be a surfer—or understands that they are surfers.

As the western world celebrated the millennium, images of surfers were everywhere. In the 1990s, one television commercial the metaphor curled home as a cool band of longboard professionals in three-piece business suits with attaché cases caught a beautiful curling brick-and-asphalt wave down Wall Street. *Esquire* ran a couple of spreads on wetsuited corporate executives ("Chairmen of the Board" and "Surfin' MBAs") with the cover call-out "Welcome, Chalk People, to the coolest scene in America" (chalk people being any non-surfing, fair-skinned inlanders). Six-time World Champion and short-term *Baywatch* television star Kelly Slater pouted under a white Stetson on the cover of *Interview* magazine

Previous spread: It's been called "the wave of the millennium," and for good reason. Whipped into this Fijian beast by a "tow-in" partner on a personal watercraft (PWC), Laird Hamilton knew all along he was just one wrong move away from certain death. Shooting out the end of this wave and into the safety of the channel, he burst into tears of fright and relief. Teahupo'o, August 17, 2000. Right: It started with Big Surf in Tempe Arizona; now there are "artificial wave machines" scattered over the globe. Inset: Duncan Scott enjoys a freshwater wave at the Japan Ocean Dome. Meanwhile, Laird Hamilton was one of the first to experiment with "strap surfing" (using footstraps on the board). Here he fires off a corkscrew 360 at Off the Wall.

176

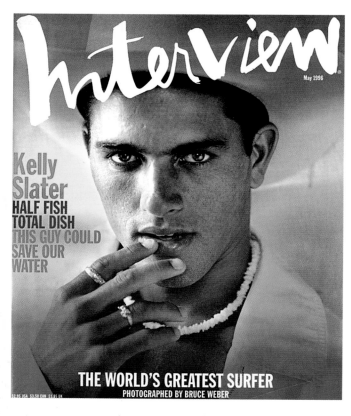

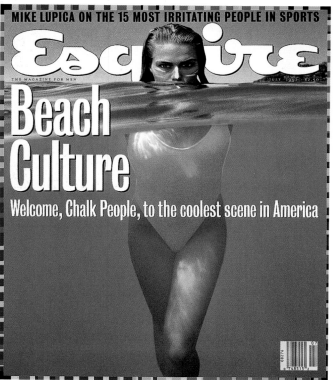

("Half Fish, Total Dish"), and *Baywatch* (that's surfing's seminal Santa Monica Bay) is just about the most popular syndicated TV show in the world. Meanwhile, Daniel Duane's *Caught Inside: A Surfer's Year on the California Coast,* Kem Nunn's *The Dogs of Winter,* and Richard Nelson's *The Island Within* received big critical acclaim in national bookstores.

< Surfing the Web >

A recent search of "surf" using my Yahoo!-brand Web browser came up with 31 categories, 1,669 Web sites, and over 8,000 listings on Yahoo! Shopping. The Web sites included the "post-punk power pop trio" Nada Surf; Club Ed: The Surf Coaching Professionals ("All Club Ed students are guaranteed to stand up and ride waves!"); Surf Gate ("The purpose of this home page is to provide an Internet presence for area churches and Christian-owned and -operated establishments"); Surf Your Watershed ("Users can locate their watersheds by text or maps and then get information"); Surf Flite ("manufacturer of skysurfing boards and wakeboards; also have instructors that provide training for each of these disciplines"); Surf Sites for CyberBiologists ("comprehensive but not overwhelming selection of sites useful for novice cyberbiologists who want to surf the biological dimension of the Web"); Yahoo! Surf Shop (T-shirts and other product sales); Yahoo!'s own "Surf School" (features "How to Surf," "Surf Guru," "Surf Lingo," and "Surf Stories," none of it related to water); Big Surf Cyber Cafe ("occupies real & cyber space. Refreshments, one dozen computers, both Mac & PC as well as a T1 connect server. Entertainment and Shopping."); Ready, Aim, Surf ("professional links for librarians"); Surf Report ("statistical reporting program geared towards marketing professionals"); Cyber Surf Wear ("casual apparel for the entire family, featuring T-shirts and sweats"); Surf Cincinnati Waterpark ("over ten waterslides and attractions, Harbor Club banquet facilities, miniature golf, go-kart racing, and bumper boats"); Skrank ("free Web-zine including surf, skate, snow, sound, sex. Hottest strippers, surfers, etc. No fancy, long-wait crap—just the cutting edge interviews & graphics!"); M.I.R.V. ("San Francisco's industrial surf opera band on Poison Eye Records"); Blues Crazy Moon and the Sun Worshippers ("blues-inspired Surf-a-billy lounge tunes to tickle your ears"); The Smooths ("Check out the only official web site for the Smooths, a band which mixes the sounds of ska, surf punk, and disco"); Surfing the Self ("personal online advice from two psychologists"); Surf Touch Software ("produces touch screen web browser, and other touch-screen-based web applications like Surf Cash"), and so on. Several hundred of the sites are actually connected with riding waves. But it's mind-boggling, isn't? The biggest technological shift of our era, and the descriptive technical language is . . . surf talk. Let's go surfin'! Click-click.

< Over Your Head >

The difference between cybersurfers and real surfers is obvious. Real surfers get in over their heads. It's easy to do.

You paddle out into the ocean, you're over your head. A big set comes, you're over your head. If you get hurt, you're over your head. You're a half mile out to sea, and you're aiming down the heaving wall of a legitimate forty-foot wave, and the wind coming up the face is blowing so hard your cheeks are flapping, and the water's sucking up

the face, too, like down a storm drain, and you're not going anywhere . . . except . . . over . . . the . . . F-A-A-A-A-A-A-A-L-L-L-S-S-S, and you're way, way over your head. In fact, you're weightless, but your feet have already been whipped out of the straps (yes, your surfboard has footstraps), and you're definitely falling, splattered around by God's own firehose, tumbled until stunned all over and blacking out until you somehow break the surface to gulp some oxygenated foam and hear the closing growl of a . . . motorcycle? . . . as you see the next monster wave humping toward you, already feathering into white at the top of the five-story wall, and then you turn just in time to see a WaveRunner™ carve past, your partner dragging a rescue sled, and you grab it and hang on as he cranks the throttle, hauling you behind like a dead seal, blasting over the shoulder of the most giant wave you've ever seen,

Surfing is the ultimate metaphor, and everyone seems to be getting it. Slater on the cover of Interview. *"Beach Culture" on the cover of* Esquire *(Art Brewer's cover shot). Everyone was surfing the Web in Y2K, but the newly popularized mega-spot near San Francisco had grown men crying for their mothers. Nothing virtual about this ride—Peter Mel (above) at Mavericks.*

179

just in the nick of time. That's a good wipeout, tow-in style. Strap-surfing style. Psycho style, hero style, no-big-thing style.

Surfing has always been about pushing the limits, from the ten-second noserides of David Nuuhiwa back in the '60s, to the five-second tuberides of Shaun Tomson, Rabbit Bartholomew, and Californian Davey Miller in the '70s, to the twenty-five-foot waves of Waimea, Makaha, and Third Reef Pipeline ridden by Greg Noll, George Downing, Pat Curren, Reno Abellira, Owl Chapman, Mark Richards, Ken Bradshaw, Mark Foo, Brock Little, Derrick Doerner, and a couple hundred others. But contemporary interest and participation in surfing at its most extreme is without precedent.

Big surf has long been one of the attractions of the Hawaiian Islands, but recent discoveries in other lands and oceans have created a virtual world big-wave circuit. Isla Todos Santos, a short boat trip off the northern Baja coast, was discovered by Windansea clubbies in the summer of 1964. But when then–World Champ Tom Curren, Dave Parmenter, and friends visited in February of 1987, they surfed the biggest waves yet photographed on the West Coast, shaking Hawaii's preeminence in the big-surf arena.

Then, in the '90s, the lid was blown off a top-secret big-wave spot in Northern California. First sampled by Half Moon Bay local Boyd Scofield in the winter of 1969–70, "Mavericks" was surfed solo by Jeff Clark, another local boy, between 1975 and 1990, the year a few friends began to join him. When coverage in *Surfer* suggested the spot was heavier than Waimea, the big-name big-wave riders had to try it for themselves. That's how it happened that North Shore veteran Mark Foo, after surviving years of big surf (including one historic forty-five-foot close-out wave at the Bay), dove off his board while dropping down the face of a relatively sedate eighteen-footer at Mavericks (December 23, 1994) and was discovered a couple of hours later, drowned at the end of his surf leash. Dozens of waves were ridden, while Foo, who'd flown in with Ken Bradshaw on the red-eye the night before, floated in the unfamiliar cold of the dark green water—bigger waves, ridden by less-experienced surfers—but it was his time, friends said later. At least he died doing what he loved.

When experienced big-wave rider Donnie Solomon died at Waimea a year later (to the day and the hour December 23, 1995) after Foo, that was a little spooky, but when big-hearted, twenty-eight-year-old North Shore veteran Todd Chesser drowned on February 13, 1997, at Outside Alligators (near Waimea), caught inside and held under by a big set, it seemed downright eerie.

In the big-waves theater of survival, the definition of stoke is twisted and stretched. Cold-water monster at Mavericks in Northern California. Some guys love this place.

The renewed fascination with riding significant waves comes with risks. A few hours after arriving on the red-eye from Honolulu in December of 1994, longtime North Shore big-wave surfer Mark Foo drowned after wiping out on a mid-sized wave at Mavericks near Half Moon Bay, California. His surfboard was spotted drifting, and Foo was discovered dead at the end of the

"In recent years, Chesser was finding it more and more difficult to stay ahead of the crowds," wrote *Surfer* field editor Ben Marcus in his report on the incident, "and he watched with growing depression as his happy hunting ground, the outer reefs, swarmed with serious big-wave surfers and tow-in wannabes. In the past year, Chesser had even discussed the unthinkable: moving away from the North Shore for good. He was engaged to a California girl . . . and looked forward to . . . a normal adult life on the Mainland. . . . A few days after his nightmare experience, Cody Graham [who survived the same set and had tried to save Chesser] had had enough: 'I'm over it. I quit. I left my big-wave board at the beach that day and just walked away. Todd Chesser was solid as a rock. He was one of the fittest men on the North Shore. I don't know why he drowned and I didn't. I came that close to going with him. I quit.'"

leash. It was his first time to surf Mavs. On the wave after Foo's, first-timers Brock Little and Mike Parsons were swept onto the inside rocks, trapped, pummeled, and almost drowned too. Sequence: Mark Foo's last wave at Mavericks; although not especially huge, the wave proved utterly fatal. Opposite: Santa Cruz surfer Jay Moriarty made his reputation at Mavericks. He was young and bold and in seriously good shape. In June of 2002, he died in a free-diving accident during a routine training session in deep water in the Maldives. A week and a half later, hundreds of surfers (including his wife) surrounded an outrigger canoe near his home at Pleasure Point for the scattering of Jay's ashes. Such is a rite of passage in surf culture.

"I think that they're towing themselves into waves that are bigger than man can survive in," says John Severson. "A lot of people are gonna die because I know, from personal experience, there's only so much that you can stand. There's only so long you can stay down, in the best of shape . . . but I think it's just incredible! To come down one of those big waves and see that wall in front of you pitching out, blocking out the sky . . . and making it! But you don't have any options if you make a mistake, and it may be your life. But life's getting cheaper; there's a lot of us."

In June 2001, Santa Cruz's youngest big-wave surfer and favorite son, Jay Moriarty (who made his reputation with a spectacular "crucifixion" wipeout in '94), drowned in a free-diving accident during routine big-wave training in the Maldives. Moriarty's extraordinary Santa Cruz memorial—hundreds of surfers surrounding an outrigger canoe off Pleasure Point for the scattering of his ashes—argued that the tribe placed a high value, indeed, on one of its own.

While inevitable conflicts arose between tow-in surfers and "paddle" surfers over issues as diverse as territory and aesthetics, milestones continued to be established. In January of 1991, a crew of big-wave surfers and camera operators motored one hundred miles straight west of San Diego, where Peter Mel, Mike Parson, Brad Gerlach, and Ken "Skindog" Collins rode the fifty-foot waves breaking on Cortes Banks, a shallow patch of reef far out of sight of any land.

< Tow-In Surfing >

Tow-in surfing is the sport's most extreme leading edge, but, like everything, it evolved a step at a time. For years surfers talked about riding the outer reefs—the "unridden realm" of waves breaking farther out to sea than any of the regular surf spots. But a 25- to 30-foot wave seemed about the limit of what a surfer could ride. It had to do with the speed of the wave, the speed a surfer could paddle, and the speed of the wind and water moving up the face of the wave against him. At a certain size, it was impossible for the surfer to make it down the wave before the wave crashed over on top of him.

But if you *pull* a guy into such an impossible wave using a boat of some kind, or one of those JetSki-type things, you just might have the board-speed to pick up the wave a lot sooner, when it's still building towards vertical. With this kind of JATO (jet-assisted take-off), it might be possible—if you don't make a mistake. And if there were footstraps on the board, the moguls of chop that would normally lead to sure wipeouts would be ramps to blast over, the way windsurfers do.

It was windsurfers who started putting straps on their sailboards, and it was windsurfers who first rode Hawaii's giant outer-reef waves. Laird Hamilton, Buzzy Kerbox, and Derrick Doerner began

A hard-core group of surfers have armed themselves with the technological toys required to tow one another into the giant waves that break on Hawaii's outer reefs. As their tow-in partners roar off on their PWCs, Laird Hamilton and David Kalama let loose their tow lines with enough speed to catch this giant wave, just as it begins to lift up over the reef at Jaws on Maui.

using a Zodiac to tow each other into outer-reef waves off the North Shore, where only extraordinary windsurfers like Robby Naish had ridden before. Being powered into a wave by a sail was like being towed in, but if you were towed in, you didn't have to contend with the sail once you were surfing. Over on Maui, windsurfers Mike Waltze, Dave Kalama, Rush Randle, Josh and Mark Angulo, and Peter Cabrinha were beginning to sail a big-wave spot called "Jaws." Hamilton and Kerbox became aware of what the Maui windsurfers were doing about the time Bruce Brown and his *Endless Summer II* crew were in the Islands hoping to do an outer-reef segment for the film. So it all came together: surfboards, surfers, outer reefs, windsurfers, straps, WaveRunners, cameras, and giant waves. Jaws became a kind of millennial Waimea, and images of surfers on 40-foot waves—hair-raising, and so recently impossible—danced on movie screens and called surfers on to greater challenges still.

An apex of sorts was reached on August 17, 2000, when Laird Hamilton was towed into a mutant aberration at Teahupo'o in Tahiti, a wave so thick and powerful that it sucked the water in front of it down to fifteen feet below sea level. As the monster barrel poured onto the shallow, draining reef off Fiji, one small mistake would have certainly cost Hamilton his life. Skating out to the camera boat after his ride, surfing's ultimate "hellman" burst into tears of relief. Never again, he seemed to be saying . . . until next time. The ride was immediately described as "the heaviest wave ever ridden."

The big-wave and outer-reef playgrounds are on a different scale—far more powerful and vast than anything surfed before. (Left) PWC pilot Dave Kalama has just towed Laird Hamilton into this Jaws wave and is racing towards the recovery position. Above: This is the Maui JATO (jet-assisted take-off) crew, including Laird Hamilton, Gerry Lopez, and several former windsurfers with appetites for riding the huge waves at Jaws, the most famous strap-surfing spot (note the straps on the surfboards) in the world.

< Surf Expression >

Previous spread: Each generation pushes the performance envelope further into the impossible realms. The son of a great surfer and one himself, then a great windsurfer, involved in the initial exploration of this giant-wave surf spot, Laird Hamilton in the straps at Jaws, making history in 1995. This is truly theater of the extreme. It is not at all like surfing the Web.

In the 1990s, surf art entered a golden age in which the meeting of man and wave inspired expressions in virtually every medium imaginable. Just as surfers like Kalani Robb (below) were finding new ways to express themselves in the waves, artists who surfed found growing interest in what they had to show and tell.

A subculture is in part defined by its language. In the beginning, a gremlin was a mischievous trouble-maker and not truly a surfer. But then the term became one of affection, almost, in gremmie, and when the Australian influence swept in, suddenly they weren't gremmies, they were grommets. It's a language that is always stretching in at least three ways: to describe new territory, for sub-tribal differentiation, and to absorb outside influence (the cultural walls are quite permeable, and as much flows in as flows out).

Surfers today talk of "ramps," "ollies," "shack time," "A-frames," "barneys," and an entire lexicon of general and specific terms that are more or less meaningful depending on your proximity to the subculture, or the sub-subculture. But the language includes the experience, too—the small acts and the big moves, the lifestyle accoutrements, the surfboards and the art. The language includes the images of a pantheon of photographers, from Blake to Ball to Brown to Maki to Grannis to Stoner to Brewer to Wilkings to Divine to a hundred hot trigger-fingers (and eyes) at work every day, building the dictionary of surfing's visible vocabulary. And the language includes written narratives, the words of everyone from Cook, Twain, and London to Matt Warshaw, Phil Jarratt, Dave Parmenter, Nat Young, Craig Stecyk, Mickey Dora, and a thousand more eloquent articulators of the sublime and the ridiculous.

The language includes the places, too, from Waikiki to Malibu, and from G-Land to J-Bay, and from Galveston and Gilgo Beach to Mavericks and Jaws. And the vehicles: *olo* and *alaia,* plank and cigar box, hot curl and Malibu chip, pop-out and custom, elephant gun and noserider, vee-ottom and mini-gun, twin-fin and thruster, longboard and shortboard.

The language of surfing is expressed and enlarged by its artists, who draw creative juice from the waves they ride, from John Severson, whose jazzy, cartoonish early work evolved into idealized tropic psychedelia; to Rick Griffin, whose incredible illustrations took him to fame outside the surfing world; to Bill Ogden, whose wonderful neo-nouveau lines and '60s themes brought life to *Surfer* ads; to Phil Roberts, who added a draftsman's precision to a wild gift for caricature; to Ken Auster's plein-air interpretations of classic surf photos; to Jessica Dunne's Hopperesque canvasses; and the consummate graffiti of TWIST, the trippy quickie surf sequences of Russell Crotty, the brilliant California landscapes of John Comer. . . . The list goes on and on. Clearly, the experience of surfing is stimulating, continuously evoking the artistic vocabulary of the surfer and the near-at-hand. The work of so many artists suggests why so many surfers argued that wave-riding was an art, not a sport, back in the early '70s.

And of course, the language includes the names: Duke, Freeth, Blake, Doc Ball, Whitey, Woody, Hoppy, Granny, Simmons, Quigg, Velzy, Bud, Dora, Fain, Yater, Doyle, Dewey, Lance, Corky, Butch, Wally, George (and George, because there are at least two Georges), Peck, Peter Pan, Morey, Murph and Murphy, Midget, Nat, Cooper, Hap, Sweet, Curren (the dad and the two sons), Joyce, Joey (two males and a female), Margo, The Surf Star Formerly Known As Kong, Rabbit, Buggs, Buffalo, Margo,

Surfer founder Severson continued to create in paint and canvas as demand for his work rose steadily in recent years. Here, in Discovery, *he celebrates the archetypical search for perfect waves.*

191

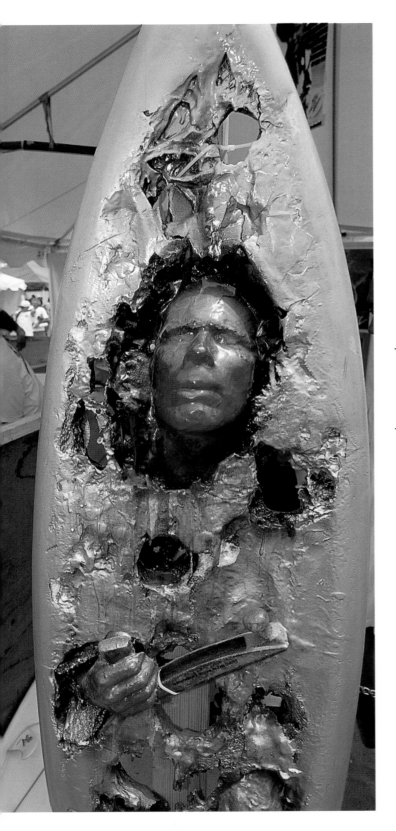

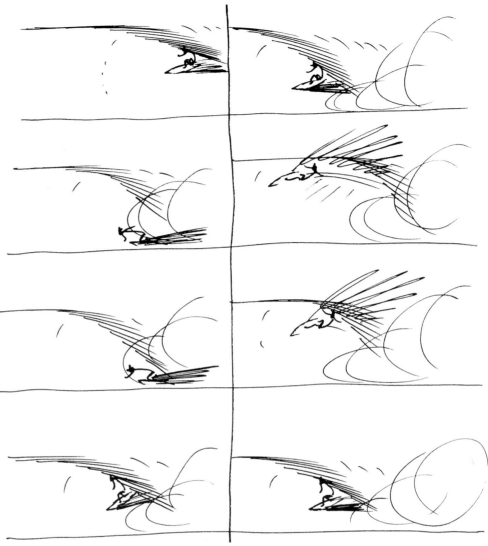

Surfboard shaper John Casper departs from the builder's craft to expose another side of the art of surfing in Huntington Beach *(left)*. Above: This Russell Crotty sketch of a tube-ride sequence beautifully captures the energy and nuances of an intense surfing experience; only a surfer could find these lines.

The Waterman *(opposite)* is typical of Malcolm Wilson's stupendous constructions, each of which are highly prized by collectors. Combining intricate scale models of classic surfboards, oodles of interesting information, and an exquisitely detailed 3D rendering of an actual surfing locale *(in this case, Dana Point before the breakwall and harbor destroyed it)* yields an extraordinarily pleasing artistic statement.

Following spread:

Three artists' visions of stoke: Top left: Trestles, *by Ken Auster, captures the sublime sense of being there; he uses a rich, plein-air watercolor palette to re-create essential photographic images on canvas; many of his works adorn Chart House restaurants. Bottom left: Steve Valiere's* Seekers *surreally embroiders and amplifies a moment familiar to all surfers—that first glimpse of the surf; his palette is as lush and wild as the tropical secrets he's describing. Right: As is his forte, Sandow Birk's* Et in Arcadia Ego *hilariously echoes the masterwork that inspired it, perfectly capturing one of the fundamental drams of surf culture. This guy's family clearly doesn't think he's ready for Pipeline.*

194

Lynn Coleman's Surf City Here We Come *blends sun, surf, and satiric wit in a raucous display of color in which each object is hyperbolically extracted from the realm of the literal, giving it a childlike sense of abandonment.*

Shaun, Owl, McTavish, RB, BK, PT, MR, Pottz, Kelly, Lisa, Sonny, Occy, and on and on, like some kind of strange, living sea scroll.

While its vocabulary includes the literature and lore promulgated in books and magazines, surf culture (and surfing itself) remains a substantially oral tradition, its information shared on the beaches and out in the lineups, its tales told around campfires or in restaurants or bars after grueling sessions or in the midst of insufferably long lulls in the surf. Beyond all the language, surfing remains what it is, and that's always changing.

196

Pamela Neswald's Night Rush, *on the other hand, is a different sort of dreamscape in which all is poised before the plunge and surfing becomes a cosmic rite of passage.*

< State of the Art >

Now there are surf camps, comfortable though spartan retreats in hailing distance of many of the world's great waves. Throughout tropical island chains, fleets of varyingly commodious yachts shuttle surf travelers out to the shoulders of splendid, remote tropical surf spots to spend weeks there, feasting on good food and perfect waves. There are surfboards that use advanced composite technology to create longer-lasting, more environmentally sound surfboards. There are surfboard auctions where boards built with the old technology in the '50s and '60s go for $2,000 or $3,000, an original hot-curl might bring $50,000 and an original Tom Blake in mint condition even more. Typical of old shapers in new demand, Dale Velzy makes fifteen boards a week (from start to finish, shaping, glassing, the works)—"bump boards, reproductions, everything"—for the Japanese market and for private collectors, mostly to be hung on walls as works of art.

Today, there are a number of surf museums celebrating the history of the sport, art galleries and shows devoted to its art and artifacts, and restaurants celebrating its theme. There are woody clubs and woody rallies celebrating the classic surf cars and huge auctions where old surfboards and memorabilia create feeding frenzies among the culture's fat cats. There are craftsmen (like Pat Curren and Malcolm Wilson) making miniature reproductions of classic surfboards and even miniature dioramas of vintage-era beaches and piers. There is a Waterman's Ball and an annual Surf Legends gathering, convening the sport's elder statesmen at a different fabulous beach each year.

There are surf magazines in Japan, England, Ireland, South Africa, France, Spain, Canada, Brazil, Sweden, New Zealand, and probably a few other countries you wouldn't expect. In the United States, the two dominant surfing periodicals (*Surfer* and *Surfing*) are owned by the same multinational conglomerate—Primedia. Hundreds of surf videos are made and marketed every year, keeping the global tribe tuned into the latest, while dozens of Web sites have replaced the coconut wireless, keeping the surf world up to the minute as hundreds of surveillance cameras transmit images of real-time surf conditions to a high-tech clientele of wave-hunters. Surfing is huge, as the success of the Hollywood film *Blue Crush* (2002) amply attests. Along with the flood of surfing images and information, surfing music has come back, big time, even though most of the bands playing it have never been near an ocean, Butthole Surfers and an ageless Dick Dale notwithstanding.

Greg Noll, who sold fifty old boards for fifty bucks apiece before he moved north to Crescent City, California, to become a commercial fisherman in the '70s and '80s, is now making about a dozen *olo* reproductions a year, selling them to collectors for up to ten thousand dollars each. "The first was red cedar," he says. "In three days of working it down, I burnt the armature out of

With five-pound surfboards, three fins, leashes, and intensified competition, the level of surfing performance has risen steadily in the past couple of decades. However, among the top pros and the gifted independents (like Hamilton), the level is absolutely ridiculous. In a word, "sick." Shown here is Andy Irons of Kauai, the 2002 ASP World Champion at 24, and as smooth a surfer as ever behaved so cruelly to a wave. Five years before this, Kelly Slater was untouchable, but such gaps always and inevitably close.

my Porter Cable power planer, one of the toughest on the market, and it still took six kids to get it [the wood blank] on the car and home to finish." The finished board (and subsequent ones) was the same dimensions as a koa wood *olo* discovered in a burial cave on Kauai. "The Hawaiians had to go up into the hills, fell the tree with a stone adze, smooth it with sand, and get it down to the water from the mountains—all without wheels!" he marvels. Yes, respect for the old ways was being maintained.

The three-fin thruster may be here to stay, but so is the longboard. "Today, 65 years later, many surfers are rediscovering their heritage just as Duke did," wrote soul surfer David Parmenter. "The biggest trend in surfing today is a worldwide shift to the longboard. You can scream and rant and bang your head on the floor, you can scrawl hate with wax on the sidewalk, you can send seething letters to the editor about fat old kooks on logs . . . but it won't change the evident fact that, demographically, longboarding is modern surfing. Or, more exactly, postmodern surfing" ("Epoch-alypse Now: Postmodern Surfing in the Age of Reason," *The Surfer's Journal,* Vol. 4, No. 4).

Even so, territory is an issue—and not just longboarders vs. shortboarders, but outsiders vs. locals (a term usually self-defined)—to the point where the phrase "wave rage" or "surf rage" has become part of the vocabulary. While precedent-setting legal actions have punished the most extreme cases, localism and violence among surfers has reached epidemic proportions, as evinced by the book *Surf Rage,* in which Nat Young (a highly visible victim of surf-related assault) and others discuss the issue. "Hopefully, we can do something about this violence," Young writes. "None of it reflects the true Spirit of Surfing. Surf rage is an ugly reality to most surfers. We've ignored it for a long time. Now it's time we took a closer look at ourselves."

In the vortex of all this energy, competitive surfing wears a new and extreme face. Concentrated pockets of population have coalesced an astute competitive consciousness in the technologically privileged youth who strive for the professional ranks. Armed with ultralight gear, they enter sunlit arenas where they create gymnastic performances that transcend the liquid medium they appear to celebrate. The airshow competitions concocted by surfers Shawn Barney Barron and Skip Snead are now a worldwide phenomenon, pointing the way to a multidimensional surfing future. In the opening years of the new millennium, a core group of intrepid surfers is set on pushing the envelope much, much further. Under the flag of the Billabong Odyssey, this elite party of big-wave surfers has embarked on a worldwide quest to ride a 100-foot wave. After all that happened in the twentieth century, what unimaginable things will be achieved by surfers in the twenty-first?

In the last decade, the surfing world has expanded. What with crowds and commotion, and the vagaries of swell and wind and tide, not to mention basic wanderlust and itchy feet, it's an ever shifting palette. So the search is never-ending, and priorities align themselves accordingly. In search of blue and white perfection in a field of green, surfers head to the office in Catanduanes, the Philippines.

The vast majority of surfers never compete. Instead, as if their attention is fixed on some true prize, they chase after waves, surf with their friends, work on their moves, ply their art, and live the life wherever they happen to be. Some seek out solitude and bear the discomforts that go with it, surfing the frigid waters of America's Pacific Northwest coast, Scotland's remote islands, or the outlands of Tasmania and Namibia. Millions of kids relate through their sponges (Boogie-style soft bodyboards), assimilating the wisdom of wave motion and absorbing the sheer magnificence and beauty of the spinning waves, playing in nature's most brilliant playground.

Snowboarding, skateboarding, windsurfing, kite surfing, strap surfing, wakeboarding, sky surfing, and other spin-off boardsports and their related cultural styles have their roots in the sport of Hawaiian kings. As a financial news commentator said on MSNBC in 2002: "There's a mass migration underway—from ball sports to board sports."

The Stoke

Surfing ocean waves is exquisite play, and the surfers who ride them plug into a whole different reality, one that is so entirely experiential that, naturally, words fail to describe it. How could anything of a play-nature be better? You're riding curling echoes of winds and storms transformed into kinetic water-sculptures at the edges of the sea. You're cavorting in these perfect spiraling three-dimensional laid-on-their-sides little tornadoes, skating down the zippering wall of the tube in the center of the cyclone. Havin' fun.

As Nat Young once said: "Riding waves daily or consistently, and taking it seriously enough, you run the risk of becoming totally surf-stoked. Once you experience this phenomenon, you can lose connection with anything and everything except your peers down on the beach, and the values the waves and ocean force upon you, whether you like it or not."

The eye of the storm, and not a drop out of place—former World Champ Derrick Ho streaking out of a tunnel of love at Pipeline. Above: A laugh from the past— Bob Cooper in Australia, 1970.

< Surf Drunk >

Even as surf culture expands at its ever youthful roots (the biggest surfing magazines target a twelve- to fifteen-year-old demographic), there is maturing respect for the old ways and the tribe's elders, an appreciation that people who have surfed all their lives have stories to tell and wisdom to impart. In 1997, hot-curl surfer Wally Froiseth, still "surf drunk" in his seventies, said he reckoned the appeal of surfing is being in nature—the challenge and, of course, standing up. "My folks used to tell me, don't stand up, it's too dangerous." How right they were.

Wally was a key man in designing the *Hawaiiloa,* a 62-foot double-hulled Polynesian voyaging canoe built from logs donated by the Tlingit, Haida, and Tsimpshian tribes of Southeast Alaska. The 200-foot-tall trees were 7 feet in diameter and more than 400 years old.

The Pipeline is the archetype of the perfect surfer's wave, so ideal at times that it almost mocks reality. How could something as transient and ineffable as a wave continue to articulate such a specific natural syllable so precisely over so many years? How, year after year, do infinite variables combine to yield these recurring perfect chords? Victor Lopez enjoys an evening wave, a kind of moon dance.

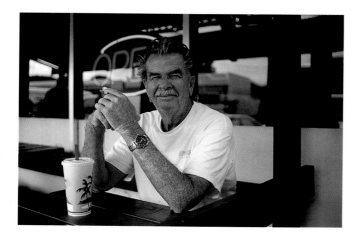

The afterglow of a life of surfing energizes the culture's senior population. Top: Surfer/shaper Mike Diffenderfer, not long before he took his leave. And Woody Brown, still surfing and smiling in January 2001 at age 89. Opposite: Late afternoon session at the Banzai Pipeline. Nothing short of magic happens here.

"They were spruce, cut off at the top," said Froiseth. "They shaped 'em out and made 'em into sailing canoes. They sailed to Tahiti, the Marquesas, then they shipped 'em up to Seattle, and we went up there to show 'em the results, and they were really happy. They treated us like kings."

Froiseth had the honor of captaining *Hawaiiloa* on the last leg of her journey from Ketchikan to Juneau in 1995. Froiseth and George Downing have kept every important surfboard they ever made and surfed—safely stashed away. Respect for the old ways is being maintained.

Woody Brown (record-setting glider pilot in the '30s, hot-curl pioneer in the '40s, creator of the modern catamaran in the '50s) still surfs the winter waves at Kahului Harbor, across the street from his Maui condo. Summers, his younger friend Wayno Cochran takes him over to the south side. "I still surf for my health, but it's not as important as before," Woody says. "Love is what's important. We have to stop killing each other."

Some surfers paddle out into the water carrying with them an enormous sense of the sport's history. They have a sense of time, an appreciation of the elemental beauty of their encounter with the waves. They know they stand at the top of a ladder that has been built over generations, but that the essential reality remains the same: man and wave. Like Northern California surfer Dale Webster (who's taken on the personal goal of surfing a full lunar cycle)—three good rides a day for 28.25 years, over 10,000 consecutive days! Inspired by his friend, the late Rick Griffin, Webster is relentless. Meanwhile, he and a few friends have created Project 7, an attempt to restore the integrity of the Russian River watershed and consequently the beach and offshore environment where he surfs. Politicians in Sacramento see these guys as crackpots, but they persist. That's what surfers are trained to do. Especially when there are waves at stake.

When *Surfer* correspondent Matt George asked Webster if he ever had moments of weakness, Dale responded: "You mean moments when I want to quit? When I want to get a real job? When I want to give up? When I wonder what on Earth have I done with my life for the past twenty years, of all the money and the jobs and the waves that I have been through . . . how could I do this to my wife, to my daughter, to my health, to my future? Why on Earth do I surf every day? Because surfing is the

ultimate explanation of what to do with our short visit here on Earth. It is the solution to what to do with waves, just as man figured out how to fly in the sky. It is an incredible union with the universe—a mainline to all that exists in this world that is bigger than man himself . . . and I epitomize what I speak."

Although the public image of surfers is often that of "duh"-speaking knuckle-draggers, some of the most eloquent, visionary, and inspiring people in the world are surfers. Midget Farrelly is a good example. Asked "What is your goal in surfing?" in an interview in 1968, Midget's response was, in part, "The genuine surfer cannot afford too much fame. The genuine surfer cannot afford to be isolated in his own break. The genuine surfer cannot afford to look after a million dollars. The genuine surfer cannot afford to dominate competition. He becomes an unfortunate, pathetic object of people's attentions when he does. The surfer must be pure, hard, calculating, precise. He must be a combination of a spartan athlete, a technologist, a futuristic spaceman of the waves. Not so much an image hero, millionaire, champion and success. This is the psychology he must take on if he is to truly succeed within himself in surfing."

It's like Dr. Timothy Leary said: "It's perfectly logical to me that surfing is the spiritual aesthetic style of the liberated self. And that's the model for the future" (*Surfer*, January 1978).

At its best, surfing remains play—easy play or big serious play—and that is the meaning that this unshakable word—*stoked!*—keeps before us. *Sport* is way too mindless a word for what surfing is, and *art* is way too complementary to the vast majority of surfers. *Martial art* might locate it best in the body-mind continuum, since surfing has many of the self-development qualities sought by seekers of one kind or another. Yes, surfing is like Aikido.

But a surfer is a different sort of creature, too, a natural athlete who lives much of his or her life outside the ordinary boundaries of society and civilization. Addicted to the juice inherent in the wave-riding experience, the surfer undergoes a transformation into a feverish and joyful state of consciousness that makes him unfit for genteel society, until he's been satisfied. The stoke of surfing is one of those wordless conditions that you have to experience to know—wordless but powerful, since it is the invisible center around which all surf culture orbits.

Masterpiece Theater: Loge seating for the winter show at Waimea Bay—one of the best views of big-wave surfing in the world.

Following spread: Rock dancers at Steamer Lane, Santa Cruz, 1989.

*Surfing is magic—riding liquid echoes of cosmic energy
at the wild fringes of continents.*

< Epilogue >

In 1969, Mickey Dora said goodbye to California, committing himself to a nomad's life:

"During a multitude of years on the California Coast, I've watched the once dominant individuals of our art phased out by an uncomprehending bureaucracy. In an apparently useless endeavor, I devoted my energies and thoughts to warn the unenlightened of the plight of the times. Now, the 'hardened' life-guards, the oldies but uglies, and the thousands of other plebeian fruit flies that compose the alleged surfing sub-sub-culture are forcing me to seek greener pasture. . . . The people who are to endure this onslaught of insanity must take positive action. Acts of juvenile destruction, such as the recent surf movie rioting, produce detrimental results. Individuals must no longer complain of oppressive conditions; they are obliged by their conscience to actively seek a better life. A renaissance of the original pioneering must force discovery of new breaks and unexplored coasts of other continents. Unknown regions of tropical splendor await the adventurous person. Darwin's theory of survival of the fittest is once again the rule of the game." (Mickey Dora, "The Crackerjack Conspiracy," *Surfer,* May 1969)

In 1989, Mickey Dora wrote from the Namibian Desert on the coast of southwest Africa:

"What better place to end one's life than in Primordial Africa? By adopting my particular type of self-imposed exile I can outdistance these scourges of mankind: those who believe in consciousness without existence and those who believe in existence without consciousness—these caricatures who go to ludicrous lengths to assert their own importance, their own grotesque, overblown ambition. . . . I wonder what the ancient Hawaiians would think of today's world. The once-prodigious, noble Hawaiian Enlightenment, with all its virtues, tribal loyalties and irrecoverable surfing skills, has in the end availed them nothing. Africa represents a last chance for the Human Spirit; one of its few remaining opportunities to return to the place from whence it came. . . . I've been globe-trotting since the age of three months. Getaway is the name of the game, and I've been burning up the road ever since. The flames are in my blood permanently." (Mickey Dora, "Million Days to Darkness," *Surfer,* July 1989)

In the end, Mickey Dora returned to his father's Montecito, California, home, where he succumbed to cancer on January 3, 2002.

THE END

216

"One of the best ways of describing what we're doing . . . is to define our roles as 'evolutionary surfers.' Everything is made of waves. At the level of electrons and neutrons. . . . Historical waves—cultural waves. The more you think about the evolutionary process, the more you see the fundamental structure of nature itself. It's the quantum theory . . . dealing with quantum leaps and quantum waves . . . things come packaged in sequential, cyclical, moving, ever-changing forms." (Timothy Leary, "The Evolutionary Surfer," *Surfer,* January 1978)

< Acknowledgments >

Steve Pezman, who has greased the wheels of our universe and keeps us all connecting and connecting and connecting.

For their gracious assistance: Dr. John Ball, Art Brewer, Bruce Brown, DeSoto Brown, Woody Brown, James Cassimus, Jeff Divine, Pierce Flynn, Wally Froiseth, Leroy Grannis, Glenn Hening, Kit Horn, Archie Kalepa, Don Kremers, Gary Lynch, Charlie Lyon, Greg MacGillivray, Alain Mazer, Greg Noll, Craig Peterson, Joe Quigg, Lori Rick, John Severson, Allan Seymour, Craig Stecyk, Bruce Sutherland, Dale Velzy, Matt Warshaw, Jeff Werve, Reynolds Yater, Nat Young.

And to my wife Susan, my son Alex, and my daughter Alana for all their love and patience.

< Bibliography >

Alpers, Antony. *Legends of the South Seas*. New York: T. Y. Crowell, 1970.

Babitz, Eve. "Surf's Up: The Artist Outlaw Who Turns Rainbow Fades into Lucky $135 Stars." *Rolling Stone*, June 20, 1974.

Baker, Bernie. "Perils of the Tropics." *Surfer Magazine*, vol. 11, no. 5, November 1970.

Bingham, Hiram. *A Residence of Twenty-One Years in the Sandwich Islands*. New York: Converse, 1847.

Bird, Isabella L. *The Hawaiian Archipelago: Six Months Amongst the Palm Groves, Coral Reefs, and Volcanoes of the Sandwich Islands*. London: John Murray, 1876.

Blair, John. *The Illustrated Discography of Surf Music, 1959–1965*. Riverside, California: J. Bee Productions, 1978.

Blake, Tom. *Hawaiian Surfboard*. Honolulu: Paradise of the Pacific Press, 1935.

Carroll, Nick, ed. *The Next Wave*. New York: Abbeville Press, 1991.

Crawford, Carin. "Waves of Transformation." Internet essay, published June 1993. http://facs.scripps.edu/surf/wavesof.html

Daws, Gavan. *Shoal of Time: A History of the Hawaiian Islands*. New York: Macmillan, 1968.

Duane, Daniel. *Caught Inside: A Surfer's Year on the California Coast*. New York: North Point Press, 1996.

Edwards, Phil, with Bob Ottum. *You Should Have Been Here an Hour Ago*. New York: Harper & Row, 1967.

Farrelly, Midget, with Craig McGregor. *The Surfing Life*. New York: Arco, 1967.

Finney, Ben, and James D. Houston. *Surfing: A History of the Ancient Hawaiian Sport*. San Francisco: Pomegranate Artbooks, 1996.

Hening, Glenn R. and Maureen. *Annual Publication*. 1st edition. Oxnard Shores, California: Groundswell Society, 1997.

Jarratt, Phil. *Mr. Sunset: The Jeff Hakman Story*. London: Gen X Publishing, 1997.

Jarves, James J. *History of the Hawaiian or Sandwich Islands*. London: Edward Moxon, 1843.

Kampion, Drew. *The Book of Waves*. Santa Barbara, California: Arpel/Surfer, 1989.

Kelly, John, Jr. *Surf and Sea*. New York: A. S. Barnes, 1965.

Klein, H. Arthur. *Surfing*. Philadelphia & New York: Lippincott, 1965.

Knox, David. *Mark Richards: A Surfing Legend*. Pymble, Australia: Angus & Robertson, 1992.

London, Jack. *Cruise of the Snark*. New York: MacMillan, 1911.

Lueras, Leonard. *Surfing: The Ultimate Pleasure*. New York: Workman Publishing, 1984.

Margan, Frank, and Ben Finney. *A Pictorial History of Surfing*. Sydney, Australia: Paul Hamlyn, 1970.

Michener, James A. *Hawaii*. New York: Random House, 1959.

Noll, Greg, and Andrea Gabbard. *Da Bull: Life Over the Edge*. Bozeman, Montana: Bangtail Press, 1989.

Pearson, Kent. *Surfing Subcultures of Australia and New Zealand*. St. Lucia, Queensland, Australia: University of Queensland Press, 1979.

Pukui, Mary Kawena, and Samuel H. Elbert. *Hawaiian Dictionary*. Honolulu: University Press of Hawaii, 1971.

Severson, John, ed. *Great Surfing*. New York: Doubleday, 1967.

——. *Modern Surfing Around the World*. New York: Doubleday, 1964.

Steele, H. Thomas. *The Hawaiian Shirt*. New York: Abbeville Press, 1984.

Stern, David H., and William S. Cleary. *Surfing Guide to Southern California*. Malibu, California: The Fitzpatrick Co., 1963.

Thrum, Thomas G. *Hawaiian Folk Tales*. Chicago: A. C. McClurg, 1921.

——. *More Hawaiian Folk Tales*. Chicago: A. C. McClurg, 1923.

Toffler, Alvin. *Future Shock*. New York: Random House, 1970.

Twain, Mark. *Mark Twain's Letters from Hawaii*. New York: Appleton-Century, 1966.

——. *Mark Twain's West*. Chicago: R.R. Donnelley, 1983.

——. *Roughing It*. Hartford, Connecticut: American Publishing Co., 1872.

Van Dyke, Fred. *30 Years of Riding the World's Biggest Waves*. Santa Cruz, California: Ocean Sports International, 1988.

Warshaw, Mat. *Mavericks, The Story of Big-Wave Surfing*. San Francisco Chronicle, 2000.

——. *Surfriders*. Del Mar, California: Tehabi Books, 1997.

Wolfe, Tom. *The Pump House Gang*. New York: Farrar, Straus & Giroux, 1968.

Young, Nat. *The History of Surfing*. Angourie, New South Wales, Australia: Palm Beach Press, 1983 and 1994.

——. *Surfing Fundamentals*. Los Angeles: The Body Press, 1985.

——. *Surf Rage*. Angourie, New South Wales, Australia: Nymboida Press, 2000.

* Note: The definitions cited in this book are from *The Random House Dictionary of the English Language* (Random House: New York, 1967), a single heavy volume, which I received from John Severson on my birthday in 1969, when I was editor of *Surfer*.

* Another note: U.S. participation numbers from the "Waverider" surfing study were provided by Board-Trac, Inc., 21371 Silvertree Lane, Trabuco Canyon, California 92679; www.board-trac.com.

* *Una mas:* All uncredited interviews were with the author.

< Photo Credits >

85: *The Surfer* cover / Drew Kampion Collection
85: *The Surfer Bi-Monthly* / Allan Seymour Collection
85: *Let There Be Surf* poster / Allan Seymour Collection
86: Phil Edwards, Banzai Pipeline, 1961 / Dr. Don James
86: *Sports Illustrated,* July 18, 1966 / Allan Seymour Collection
87: *Surf Guide* magazine / Courtesy John Van Hamersveld
87: Australia's *Tracks* magazine / Courtesy *Tracks*
88: Corky Carroll ad for Keds / *Surfer* magazine
88–89: Hamm's Beer take-off by Dr. Don James / Allan Seymour Collection
90–91: Greg Noll at Pipeline, 1964 / John Severson
92: Surfer on the beach at Waimea Bay, 1977 / Drew Kampion
92–93: "The Beast" at Velzyland, 1962 / Leo Hetzel
94: David Nuuhiwa nose arch / Steve Wilkings
94: Nuuhiwa at '72 World Contest, Oceanside / Drew Kampion
94: Corky Carroll noseriding at Poche, July '65 / Ron Stoner / *Surfer* magazine
95: Morey Invitational Poster / Mickey Muñoz Collection
95: 1969 USSC Huntington Beach program / Allan Seymour Collection
95: Reno Abellira at Huntington pier, 1969 / Drew Kampion
96: *Endless Summer* crew in South Africa / Courtesy Bruce Brown Films
96: *Endless Summer* poster / Allan Seymour Collection
97: Duke Kahanamoku at '66 World Contest, San Diego / Ron Stoner / *Surfer* magazine
97: Nat Young with trophy, San Diego '66 / Ron Stoner / *Surfer* magazine
98: Joey Cabell in the ring, Peru, 1968 / Leo Hetzel
99: Nat Young at Honolua Bay, December '67 / John Witzig
100: Bob McTavish, Channel Islands, 1967 / George Greenough
101: George Greenough with Velo, 1967 / John Witzig
102: Greenough at Lennox Head, Australia, 1967 / John Witzig
103: Nat Young at Haleiwa, December '68 / Ron Stoner / *Surfer* magazine
104: Rick Griffin, Hollister Ranch, spring 1970 / Drew Kampion
104: Griffin painting the magic surf bus, Motorskill / Drew Kampion
105: Challenger Surfboards ad, 1968 / *Surfer* magazine
105: *Five Summer Stories* poster / Allan Seymour Collection
105: Dick Brewer in lotus pose / David Darling
106: Barry Kanaiaupuni at Honolua Bay, 1972 / Art Brewer
106: Bunker Spreckels at Backdoor Pipeline, '69 / Peter French
107: Owl Chapman at Maalaea, 1976 / Steve Wilkings
108: Marine confiscation 1 at Trestles, '69 / Ron Stoner
108: Marine confiscation 2 at Trestles. '69 / Drew Kampion
109: Rolf Aurness at Johanna, 1970 World Contest, Australia / Drew Kampion
109: Aurness on the beach at Malibu, summer of '69 / Brad Barrett
110: Surfers and dolphin / Rick Doyle
110–11: Honolua Bay, Maui / Jim Cassimus
112–13: Tom Carroll flyaway cutout / Steve Wilkings
114: Surfing Again! T-shirt / Mike Moir
114: Country Surfboards, Haleiwa, 1971 / Drew Kampion
115: Mike Stewart, North Shore, '92 / Rick Doyle
116–17: Kevin Naughton in Fiji / Craig Peterson
118: Steve Pezman and Timothy Leary, San Onofre, 1978 / Art Brewer
118: Sound Spectrum calendar, 1971 / Allan Seymour Collection
119: Morocco campsite, January '75 / Craig Peterson
119: *Surfer* magazine reader in Africa, 1972 / Craig Peterson
120: Jeff Hakman, North Shore, 1974 / Drew Kampion
120: Jeff Hakman, 1974 Smirnoff Pro-Am, Waimea Bay / Steve Wilkings
121: Rollin' in Mexico, 1976 / Tim Bernardy
121: Rick Rasmussen, Long Island, 1977 / Drew Kampion
121: Bunker Spreckels with red board, 1969 / Art Brewer
122: Peter McCabe at Uluwatu, 1973 / Dan Merkel

123: G-land, Java / John S. Callahan
124: Gerry Lopez at Cloudbreak, Fiji / Jeff Divine
124-25: Lopez at Pipeline (sequence), 1975 / Steve Wilkings
125: Lopez as Dayak / Courtesy Leonard Brady
126: Larry Bertlemann, Katin swimwear ad, 1973 / Art Brewer
126: "Guns" at Waimea, Smirnoff Pro-Am, 1975 / Drew Kampion
126: Wayne "Rabbit" Bartholomew, December '75 / Drew Kampion
127: The cast of *Big Wednesday* / Courtesy Leonard Brady
127: *Apocalypse Now!* napalm and surf / Courtesy Leonard Brady
128: Aikau family portrait / Steve Wilkings
128–29: Eddie Aikau at Waimea Bay, December 1973 / Steve Wilkings
130: *Free Ride* poster, 1978 / Courtesy Bill Delaney
130: Oceanside Pier contest crowd, mid-'80s / Mike Moir
131: Danny Kwock and Newport boys, c. 1987 / Mike Moir
132: Robert August Surfboard shop, 1976 / Larry Moore / *Surfing* magazine
132: Newport Wedge colors, '88 / Mike Moir
133: Haleiwa surf shop, North Shore / Rick Doyle
133: Catalina Classic poster / Allan Seymour Collection
124: Underwater thruster / Rick Doyle
135: Simon Anderson with Thruster, 1981 / Bill McCausland
136: Megan Abubo with thruster / Jeff Divine
136–37: Christian Fletcher airing at Trestles, '89 / Larry Moore / *Surfing* magazine
138–39: Mark Richards at Pipeline, Billabong Pro, January '89 / Rick Doyle
139: Santa Cruz "No Surfing Contest" statement / Jeff Divine
140–41: Santa Cruz contest crowd with judges / Drew Kampion
141: James "Booby" Jones and ABC's Bill Fleming, 1972 / Drew Kampion
142–43: Tom Carroll snap-back at Pipe Masters, '91 / Art Brewer
144–45: Sonny Garcia and throngs, '87 Op Pro, Huntington Beach / Jeff Divine
145: The Bronzed Aussies / Drew Kampion Collection
146: Mark Richards / Norman Seef / *Surfing* magazine
147: Tom Curren, Off the Wall, 1987 / Jim Russi
147: Tom and Pat Curren, 1995 / Mike Moir
148–49: Gerry Lopez at Pipeline / James Cassimus
150: The Calhouns at Makaha, 1962 / Le Roy Grannis
151: Roxy Wahine Classic poster / Allan Seymour Collection
151: Margo Godfrey at Hammonds Reef, 1967 / Ron Stoner / *Surfer* magazine
152: Margo Godfrey Oberg, Kauai, 1977 / Jeff Divine
152–53: Rochelle Ballard, North Shore, 1997 / Jeff Divine
154–55: Lisa Andersen, North Shore, 1995 / Jeff Divine
155: Lisa Andersen triptych / Art Brewer
156: Quiksilver Logo, Billabong Logo, Reef Always On Ad / Jim Oneal
156–57: Five young grommets, 1987 / Jim Russi
158: Kelly Slater and fans, Huntington Beach, 1995 Op Pro / Jim Russi
158–59: Kelly Slater, 1996 Eddie at Waimea Bay / Jim Russi
160: Nat Young longboardin', 1993 / Jim Russi
161: Glenn Hening / Courtesy Glenn Hening
161: Tom Pratte / Courtesy Glenn Hening
162: Eddie Vedder and Pierce Flynn / Courtesy Surfrider Foundation
162: *MOM* album / Courtesy Surfrider Foundation
163: Surfrider Foundation protest paddle, Adour River, France / Art Brewer
164: *Life* magazine, Dec. 10, 1951 / *Time* / *Life* magazine
164: Einstein imagination / Rick Rietveld
165: Coco Harrison / Art Brewer
165: *Surfer* magazine's *Surfers: The Movie* edition / Drew Kampion Collection
165: Mickey Muñoz—formal and informal sandals / Art Brewer
166: *Beach Culture* magazine / Robert Avellan Collection
167: The Fletcher family / Art Brewer

168–69: Crowded lineup / Rick Doyle
169: Warnings at Sunset Cliffs / Jeff Divine
170: Corky Carroll for President / Art Brewer
170: Gerry Lopez: Chairman of the Board / Art Brewer
171: Huntington Beach riot, 1986 / Sarge
172: Frog House shark art / Mike Moir
172–73: The lineup at Waimea Bay / Art Brewer
174–75: Laird Hamilton at Teahupo'o / Tim McKenna
176–77: Japan Ocean Dome, Duncan Scott, '00 / John S. Callahan
176–77: Laird Hamilton corkscrew (sequence) / Art Brewer
178: *Interview* mag's Kelly Slater cover / Robert Avellan Collection
178: *Esquire* mag's "Beach Culture" issue / Art Brewer Collection
179: Peter Mel at monster Mavericks, 2002 / Frank Quirarte
180–81: Serious energy at Mavericks / Bob Barbour
182: Mark Foo's fatal fall at Mavericks (sequence) / Robert Brown
183: Jay Moriarty memorial in Santa Cruz, June 26, 2001 / Dan Coyro
184–85: Tow-in antics at Jaws, Maui / Erik Aeder
186–87: Laird Hamilton and David Kalama at Jaws / Erik Aeder
187: The pioneer tow-in crew, Maui '95 / Erik Aeder
188–89: Laird Hamilton at Peahi Reef (Jaws), 1995 / Erik Aeder
190: Kalani Robb, face-hop, December '98 / Jeff Divine
191: *Discovery* (1978) / John Severson
192: Shaper John Caster's creation / Mike Moir
192: *Sequence Surfing Sketch* (1997) / Russell Crotty
193: *The Waterman* construction and Dana Point diorama / Malcolm Wilson
194: *Trestles* (1993) / Ken Auster
194: *Seekers* (2001) / Steve Valiere
195: *Et in Arcadia, Ego* (1989) / Sandow Birk
196: *Surf City Here We Come* (1979) / Lynn Coleman
197: *Night Rush* (2000) / Pamela Neswald
198–99: Andy Irons, North Shore, 2001 / Pete Frieden
200–201: Kasey Curtis, SoCal Secret Spot / Larry Moore / *Surfing* magazine
202: "TJ" at Velzyland / Rob Gilley
203: Catanduanes, Philippines / John S. Callahan
204: Bob Cooper, Australia, 1970 / Drew Kampion
204–5: Derek Ho at Pipeline, 1989 / Jim Russi
206: Victor Lopez at Pipeline (sequence) / Art Brewer
208: Mike Diffenderfer, Haleiwa, January 2001 / Drew Kampion
208: Woody Brown, Kahului, January 2001 / Drew Kampion
208–9: Later afternoon Pipeline, December 1978 / Drew Kampion
210–11: Waimea Bay dress circle / Rob Gilley
212–13: Rock Dancers at Steamer Lane, 1989 / Rick Doyle
214–15: Sunset celebration, / Tom Dugan
216: Dora in top hat, c.1968 / Craig Stecyk
217: Gerry Lopez at Pipeline, 1975 / Drew Kampion
218: Huntington competitor, 1969 / Drew Kampion
220: Steve Wilkings with waterphoto gear, 1977 / Drew Kampion
222: O'Neill "tuxedo" wetsuits stoke South Africa, 1976 / Tim Bernardy

Thanks to Jim Oneal for sharing his vintage decal and patch collection. You can reach him at jimoneal@earthlink.net

Thanks to Allan Seymour for opening his vault and to James Cassimus for getting the goods. For more of Allan's collection, keystroke your way to classicsurf.com

Special thanks to Bev Morgan.

< Index >

A
Abellira, Reno, 101, 106, 127, 180
Abubo, Megan, 136
Action Sports Retailer (magazine), 130–31
Aikau, Eddie, 91, 127–28
Ali, Mohammed, 74
Alter, Hobie, 23, 63–65, 86, 95
Andersen, Erica, 155
Andersen, Lisa, 153, 155, 161, 196
Anderson, Simon, 135, 146
Apocalypse Now (film), 127
Army Corps of Engineers (ACE), 161
Arness, James, 108–9
Arrambide, Brandon, 15
Art of Peace, The (treatise), 147
Association of Surfing Professionals (ASP), 146, 156, 160–61, 198
August, Robert, 26, 96, 132
Aurness, Rolf, 107–9, 145
Auster, Ken, 191, 193
Australian Surfer, The (magazine), 87
Australian Surfing Life (magazine), 122
Australian Surfing World (magazine), 87
Avalon, Frankie, 81

B
Ball, Dr. John "Doc," 25, 45, 59, 190–91
Ballard, Bill, 152
Ballard, Rochelle, 152
balsa boards, 62, 72
Band on the Run (film), 120
Barron, Shawn "Barney", 202
Bartholomew, Wayne "Rabbit," 127, 161, 180
Baywatch (television), 158, 178
Beach Ball (film), 81
Beach Blanket Bingo (film), 81

Beach Boys, 82–84, 163
Beach Culture (magazine), 166, 169, 179
Beach Party (film), 81, 82
Bellyboard, soft-foam, 95
Bertlemann, Larry, 127, 136, 156
Big Wednesday (film), 125, 127–28, 130
Billabong, 166, 169, 202
Bing Surfboards, 103
Bird, Isabella L., 34
Blake, Tom, 41–45, 48, 50, 52–53, 55–56, 59–60, 72, 162, 190–91
Blue Crush (film), 198
Blue Hawaii (film), 164–65
Body Glove, 166
Boogie Board, 95, 115, 117, 130
Boogie-style soft bodyboards, 203
Botha, Wendy, 153, 156
Boyd, Duke, 87, 125
Boyum, Bill, 123
Boyum, Mike, 123
Brewer, Richard, 99, 101, 105–6, 125, 127, 190
Bronzed Aussies, the, 145, 170
Brown, Bruce, 18, 23, 83–86, 96, 117, 170
Brown, Woody, 57, 191, 208
Browne, Bud, 59–60, 96, 117, 128, 150, 191
Buran, Joey, 20, 191
Byron Bay, Australia, 100, 105, 110, 145

C
Cabell, Joey, 91, 97–98, 170, 191
Cairns, Ian, 127–28, 145–46, 153, 155
Calhoun, Candy, 150
Calhoun, Marge, 150, 152
Calhoun, Robyn, 150

California Coastal Commission, 161
California Surfriders (film), 59
Carroll, Corky, 88, 94–95, 98, 106, 108, 141, 170–71, 191
Carroll, Tom, 114, 142, 146
Carson, Lance, 25, 72, 74, 162, 191
Caught Inside: A Surfer's Year on the California Coast (book), 178
Championship, World Surfing, first, 97
Chapin, Gard, 54–55, 74, 78
Chapman, Owl, 107, 127, 180, 196
Chesser, Todd, 180, 182
Chicago Sun-Times (newspaper), 170
chip boards, 56, 62, 64, 190
Chouinard, Yvon, 162–63
Clark, Gordon "Grubby," 23, 161–62
Clean Water Act, 162
Collins, Ken "Skindog," 182
Conan the Barbarian (film), 125
Coogan, Jackie, 54
Cook, Captain James, 34–36, 190
Cosmic Children, The (film), 105
Cross, Dickie, 52, 57, 61
Crotty, Russell, 191–92
culture, Hawaiian, 33–35, 37. *See also* Hawaiian culture
culture, Polynesian, 35, 46. *See also* Polynesian culture
Curren, Pat, 58, 61–62, 88, 147, 180, 191, 198
Curren, Tom, 147, 156, 163, 166, 180, 202

D
Dale, Dick, 81–82, 84–85, 163
Darren, James, 65
Dee, Sandra, 65, 70, 81
Delaney, Bill, 130, 165–66
Dewey Weber Surfboards, 103
Dick Dale and His Del-Tones, 81–82
Diffenderfer, Mike, 208
Discovery (painting), 191
Doerner, Derrick, 180, 185
Dogs of Winter, The (book), 178
Don't Make Waves (film), 81
Dora, Mickey or Miki, 25–26, 72, 74–75, 78, 81, 88, 106, 141, 190–91, 216
Downing, George, 52, 58, 60, 95, 97, 180, 208
Doyle, Mike, 95, 127, 132, 191
drugs, 118, 123, 132
Dukes of Hazzard (television), 142

E
Ebert, Roger, 170
Edwards, Phil, 27, 60, 64–65, 85–86, 95, 97, 99, 125
Einstein, Albert, 28, 45, 164

Endless Summer, The (film), 23, 26, 96–98, 117, 132
Endless Summer II (film), 170, 187
Esquire (magazine), 176, 179
Evans, Bob, 87, 97, 99, 122
Evolution (film), 105

F
Fain, Johnny, 26, 191
Falzon, Alby, 105, 122
Family Free (film), 122
Farewell to the King (film), 125
Farrelly, Bernard "Midget," 85, 97, 99, 106, 191, 211
Five Summer Stories (film), 105, 125, 130
Fletcher, Christian, 136, 166
Fletcher, Herbie, 2, 157, 166
Folk, Ray, 19
Foo, Mark, 180, 182
Ford, Alexander Hume, 37, 40
Fredrico, Jason, 10
Free and Easy (film), 117
Free Ride (film), 125, 130, 166
Freeman, Jim, 85, 117
Freeth, George David, 38–40, 48–49, 56, 191
Froiseth, Wally, 19, 52, 58, 60, 191, 206, 208
From Here to Eternity (film), 165
Funicello, Annette, 81

G
Gable, Clark, 107
Garcia, Sonny, 145, 196
George, Sam, 52, 191
Gidget (book), 65
Gidget (film), 65, 70, 81, 132
Gidget Goes Hawaiian (film), 81, 85
Gocher, William, 40
Godfrey, Arthur, 165
Godfrey, Margo. *See* Margo Godfrey Oberg
Gordon, Becky, 22
Gotcha Sportswear, 130, 165
Greenough, George, 87, 98, 100–102, 105, 128, 191
Griffin, Rick, 60, 104–5, 117, 169, 191, 208
Grigg, Ricky, 88, 91
Ground Swell Society (magazine), 162
Gunsmoke (television), 108–9

H
Hakman, Jeff, 120, 123, 127
Hamasaki, Joey, 152, 191
Hamilton, Bill, 114, 117, 128, 162
Hamilton, Laird, 176, 185, 187, 190
Harrelson, Woody, 163

Harrison, Lorrin "Whitey," 49, 165, 191
Hawaiian culture, 33–35, 37
Hawaiian Surfing Movie (film), 59
Hawaiiloa (canoe), 206
Hemmings Jr., Fred, 106, 142, 145–46
Henderson, "Cowboy," 26
Hendrix, Jimi, 108
Hening, Glenn, 161–62
Ho, Derrick, 204
Hobie signature model, 91
Hobie team, 170
Hoffman, Flippy, 58
Hoffman, Joyce, 152, 191
Hoffman, Walter, 57–58, 64
hollow board, 43, 45, 48, 52
Honolua Bay, 101, 107, 110
Honolulu Advertiser, The (newspaper), 115
Horan, Cheyne, 135, 145
hot-curl surfboard, 52, 190, 208; guys, 58
Hot Lips (film), 125
Hot Generation, The (film), 101
Huntington, Henry E., 38
Hynson, Mike, 26, 95–96, 98, 108

I
Illustrated Discography of Surf Music, 1959–1965, The (book), 82
In Search of Tubular Swells (film), 123
Inner Tubes (film), 125
Innermost Limits of Pure Fun, The (film), 105
International Professional Surfers Association (IPS), 142, 145
International Surfing (magazine), 87
International Surfing Federation, 97, 107, 145
Interscope Records, 163
Interview (magazine), 158, 176
Irons, Andy, 198
Irons, Ricky, 95
Island Within, The (book), 178

J
Jacobs Surfboards, 103
James, Dr. Don, 60, 88
Jarratt, Phil, 119, 122, 190
Jeffreys Bay, 110
jet assisted take-off (JATO), 185, 187. *See also* tow-in surfing

K
Kahanamoku, Duke, 39–43, 48–49, 53, 60, 62, 97
Kahanamoku, Duke, Invitational, 101, 120, 170
Kalama, David, 185, 187

Kamehameha Garment Company, Ltd., 165
Kanaiaupuni, Barry, 91, 107, 127
Kekai, Rabbit, 19, 52, 146, 191
Kelly, John, 52, 161, 196
Kerbox, Buzzy, 166, 185, 187
Kivlin, Matt, 58, 74, 78
kneeboard, spoon-shaped, 102
Kohner, Frederick "Fritz," 65, 79
Kohner, Kathy "Gidget," 65, 79, 81
kook cord, 114. *See also* leash

L
L.A. Lakers, 88
L.A. riot, 171
Leary, Dr. Timothy, 118, 211
leash, 114. *See also* kook cord
Let There Be Surf (film), 85
Life (magazine), 80, 109, 165
lifeguarding, 56
Life's A Beach, 165
London, Charmian, 37–39
London, Jack, 32, 37–40, 46
longboarders, 157, 162, 170
longboard: 101, 145, 155, 190; tours, 161
Lopez, Gerry, 101, 123, 125, 127–28, 148, 171, 187, 202
Lynch, Wayne, 101, 105, 108

M
MacGillivray, Greg, 84, 117, 128
Makaha, Hawaii, 19, 57–60, 62, 87, 91, 97, 106, 117, 139, 150, 152, 180
Makahena, Blackie, 52
Martinson, Mark, 95, 117
McCartney, Paul, 163
McTavish, Bob, 99–102, 105, 196
Mel, Peter, 179, 182
Midget Goes Hawaiian (film), 85
Milius, John, 125, 127–28
Miller, Rusty, 88, 95, 122
Morey, Tom, 115, 141, 191
Morey, Tom, Invitational, 94
Moriarty, Jay, 182
Morning of the Earth (film), 105, 122
Mossimo, 166
Muñoz, Mickey, 60–61, 74, 81, 95, 165
Murphy, 104, 191
Muscle Beach Party (film), 81, 82
Music for Our Mother Ocean (MOM), 162–63

N
National Geographic (magazine), 60
National Scholastic Surfing Association, 155
Natural Art, The (film), 105

Naughton, Kevin, 117, 119
Neswald, Pamela, 197
New Yorker, The (magazine), 166
Night Rush (painting), 197
Ninth Wave, The (novel), 65
Nixon, Richard Milhous, 108
No Fear, 166
Noll, Greg, 58, 61–62, 65, 85, 91, 104, 180, 198
Nolte, Nick, 125
North Shore. *See* Oahu, Hawaii
noserider, 95, 100, 145, 190
Nuuhiwa, David, 94–95, 105, 107–8, 145, 180

O

Oahu, Hawaii, 35, 37, 52, 58, 87, 126, 128; North Shore, 8, 57–58, 60–61, 91, 105, 107, 110, 117, 121, 125–28, 147–48, 151–152, 156, 169, 180, 182, 187
Oberg, Margo Godfrey, 150, 152, 156, 191
Occhilupo, Mark, 156, 160
Our Mother Ocean (OMO), 161
Outrigger Canoe and Surfboard Club, 37–38, 40, 95, 142, 146
Outside (magazine), 155

P

Pacific Coast Highway, 74
Pacific Vibrations (film), 104–5, 108
paddling races, 42, 62
People (magazine), 158
Petersen's Surfing (magazine), 87
Peterson, Preston "Pete," 48–50, 54, 82
Pezman, Steve, 118, 161, 166, 176
Polynesian culture, 35, 46
Pratte, Tom, 161–62
Professional Golf Association (PGA), 142

Q

Quigg, Joe, 54–56, 58, 151, 191
Quiksilver, 120, 128, 130, 156, 158, 165, 169
Quiksilver Pro, 155

R

Rainbow Bridge (film), 108
Reader's Digest (magazine), 96
Rebel Without a Cause (film), 81
Reid, Sam, 49, 53
Richards, Mark, 139, 146, 171, 180
Rick Surfboards, 103
Ride the Wild Surf (film), 74, 81
Rietveld, Rick, 164
Rindge, May Knight, 53
Rindge, Samuel K., 53
Rolling Stone (magazine), 147, 163

Roosevelt Highway, 53
Rosemberg, Tito, 117, 119
Roxy, 155
Rusty, 165

S

Sacrifice Surf (film), 85
Santa Cruz Surfing Club, 51
Save Our Surf (SOS), 161
Schwartzenegger, Arnold, 125
Sea of Joy (film), 105
Seadreams (film), 105
Seef, Norman, 171
Seekers (painting), 193
Severson, John, 17, 23, 56, 84–85, 88, 104–5, 108–9, 127, 161, 182, 191
shortboard revolution, 100, 103, 132, 157, 162, 170, 190
Simmons, Bob, 53, 55, 78, 117, 191
Slater, Kelly, 25, 141, 157–58, 161, 198
Slippery When Wet (film), 85
Smirnoff Pro-Am, 127, 141
Smirnoff, Shawn, 130
Sorrell, Ron, 142, 146
Sound Spectrum, Laguna Beach's, 119
Spencer, Ted, 101, 108
Sports Illustrated (magazine), 86, 104
Spreckels, Bunker, 107, 121
Stecyk, Craig, 94, 190
Stoner, Ron, 117, 121
strap surfing, 187, 190 . *See also* tow-in surfing
Stüssy, 165
Stüssy, Shawn, 130
Sun Also Rises, The (film), 98
Sunn, Rell, 25
Surf City Here We Come (painting), 196
surf culture, 34, 46, 48–49, 51, 56, 58, 84
Surf Fever (film), 84–85, 87
Surf Guide (magazine), 87, 96
Surf Industries Manufacturing Association (SIMA), 163
Surf-O-Rama, trade show, the, 88
Surf Rage (book), 202
Surf Trek to Hawaii (film), 85
Surfabout (magazine), 87
Surfboard: design, 56; mini-gun, 105; leash, 114; hollowed-out, 119; three-finned, 132; Thruster, 3-fin, the, 135, 190; twin-fin, 190; V-bottom Plastic Machine, 101
Surfdog Records, 163
Surfer (magazine), 23, 25, 56, 70, 78, 80–81, 84–88, 96, 98, 100–101, 104, 109, 114–15, 118–19, 121, 127, 141, 161, 169, 180, 182, 191, 198, 211, 216–17

Surfer Bi-Monthly (magazine), 87
Surfer for President (album), 170
Surfer Quarterly, The (magazine), 87
Surfers (film), 165
Surfers (magazine), 169
Surfer's Annual (magazine), 104
Surfers Against Sewage, 162
Surfers Environmental Alliance, 162
Surfer's Journal, The (magazine), 52, 171, 176, 202
Surfer's Medical Association, 166
Surfers: The Movie (film), 166
Surfing (magazine), 25, 146, 166, 169, 171, 198
Surfing Hollow Days (movie), 86, 96
Surfing Illustrated (magazine), 87
Surfrider Foundation, 161–62
Surfrider International, 163
surfwear, 164
Sutherland, Jock, 91, 98, 125, 127

T

Thruster, 3-fin, the, 135, 190
Time (magazine), 80
Tomson, Michael, 130, 171
Tomson, Shaun, 146, 180, 196, 202
tow-in surfing, 185, 187. *See also* jet assisted take-off
Townend, Peter, 127–28, 145–46, 156
Tracey, Terry "Tubesteak," 26, 75, 79
Tracks (magazine), 87, 122
Trent, Buzzy, 91
Trestles (sketch), 193
Truman, Harry, 164–65
Twain, Mark, 36, 39, 46, 190
twin-fin surfboard, 190

U

U.S. Amateur Championship, 156

V

Van Artsdalen, Butch, 91, 125, 191
Van Dyke, Fred, 91, 142, 145
V-bottom Plastic Machine, 101
Vedder, Eddie, 162, 163
Velzy, Dale, 56, 65, 72, 191, 198

W

Waikiki Beach Club, 97
Waikiki, Hawaii, 37–40, 42–43, 48, 52, 57–58, 60, 78, 95–97, 125, 142, 151, 161, 165, 171, 190
Waimea Bay, Hawaii, 4, 20, 57, 61–62, 78, 86, 92, 110, 127–28, 152, 158, 172, 180, 187, 211
Wake of the Red Witch, The (film), 41–42
Warren, Mark, 122, 127, 145

Warshaw, Matt, 171, 190
Waves of Change (film), 105, 117
Wayne, John "Duke," 41–42
Weber, Dewey, 26, 72, 191
West, Jerry, 88
Western Surfing Association, 161
Wild One, The (film), 81
Wired (magazine), 163
Witzig, John, 100–101, 108
World Championship Tour, 147, 155, 161
World Contest, 97, 100, 106, 145
World Qualifying Series (WQS), 161
World War II, 50, 54–55, 139, 151, 164

X

X-Files, The (television), 171

Y

Yater, Reynolds, 64
Young, Nat, 14, 97–103, 108, 141, 145, 157, 160, 162, 166, 190–91, 202, 204

Z

Zahn, Tom, 54, 58, 62, 82
Zamba, Frieda, 153, 156